openFrameworks Essentials

Create stunning, interactive openFrameworks-based applications with this fast-paced guide

Denis Perevalov

Igor (Sodazot) Tatarnikov

BIRMINGHAM - MUMBAI

openFrameworks Essentials

First published: April 2015

Production reference: 1140415

Published by Packt Publishing Ltd.
Livery Place
35 Livery Street
Birmingham B3 2PB, UK.

ISBN 978-1-78439-614-5

www.packtpub.com

Credits

Authors
Denis Perevalov
Igor (Sodazot) Tatarnikov

Reviewers
Cory Barr
Dmitry Philonenko
Alex Samuel

Commissioning Editor
Kunal Parikh

Acquisition Editor
Rebecca Youé

Content Development Editor
Ritika Singh

Technical Editor
Humera Shaikh

Copy Editor
Sarang Chari

Project Coordinators
Aboli Ambardekar
Judie Jose

Proofreaders
Simran Bhogal
Stephen Copestake
Ameesha Green
Safis Editing

Indexer
Hemangini Bari

Graphics
Abhinash Sahu

Production Coordinator
Nilesh R. Mohite

Cover Work
Nilesh R. Mohite

Foreword

You have chanced upon a chapter that not many will read. With a couple of phrases quoted on the cover, a foreword is quite a doubtful genre in modern technical literature. Usually, such texts begin with "the book you are holding...", but perhaps you are holding a gadget and your fingers miss the touch of coarse paper, or you are reading a nicely designed printed booklet of selected chapters from the book.

The main thing is that the book is in your hands as well as the technology, which exists in digital space only but can make most physical objects around us interactive. The book about the technology, special features, methods, and principles of work will be there on your desk among some printouts, crumpled designs, and endless paper cups that deliver portions of invigorating caffeine to us. It will be scolded by a beginner, or criticized by a professional, but it will also be bookmarked by hundreds and commented on the margins by thousands of people certainly advancing in mastering a powerful instrument of technological and creative use—openFrameworks.

This is a generation of code designers, artists with digital tools, engineers with the programmed project functionality—a young, unexpected generation, which is used to constant studying, the constant state of a novice making the first attempt to cope with a new principle and a new instrument—a fresh start. If you're part of this categorization, this book will be a great base to acquire new habits and will act as the first step towards self-development for you.

The pro goes ashore

A profession is neither a bronze molding nor a stone monument but a living and evolving form. A coder's, a programmer's, and an interactive project engineer's profession has been living until now in the depth of the office ocean among the unicellular executors of other people's plans and among the irresolute and inert workers unable to motivate themselves, to broaden the range of instruments, technologies, and wishes—wishes to exceed the environment of hired workers and step into the world of high professional competition belonging to men of business—men of solution finding.

For professionals, evolution is to consider that they are beginners again. Taking a manual and evening by evening, at home by the lamplight forging their new armor, their strong professional exoskeleton, to exceed habitual tasks allowing them to step out of an ocean of many and onto the beach of singularities where the experience of the past and the ambitions of the future change the very idea of workspace, competences, and hierarchies.

You can be an experienced coder having worked at different sites and application for years, but you have to go to the bottom studying again, doing tests and exercises, correcting amateur mistakes, getting a new experience, and changing your idea about what can be done by yourself, by your intellect, your vision, and your imagination. Changes inspire as do understanding, knowledge, and experience. A book that makes you sink down to the bottom, consuming several evenings or a couple of weeks, will eventually help you to understand a lot.

Although it is the basics, they are assembled intentionally into a compact, handy structure of informational portions, maybe not so exquisitely designed but definitely rich in nutritious and simple practical ways. This book is going to rest on the shelf after you, led by the success of consecutive learning, have performed a series of simple works based on the examples, gradually and consciously going ashore onto a new professional environment. You will enter the era of probably the most active technological education—self-education by means of hundreds of available sources.

The era of self-education

The authors of this book are professionals tired of putting on knowledge as a clumsy sea lion puts on fat. Knowledge should constantly attract new ideas, and a book is probably the best way to share it. This book is not a step but a jump. A sea lion stepped ashore out of the thick, powerful knowledge clot, stiff on the land of theoretical teaching methods and surprisingly flexible in its natural environment of project development. We witness the evolution into methodologists, teachers, and preachers of technologies.

We have stepped into the era of instant evolution of knowledge, habits, and experience, into a period of high-speed reforging and assembly of new details and completely unique professional habits. Programming inspires advertisers and artists. Mobile applications become the channels for spreading marketing and cultural novelties. Behind the glossy interface design, there are people following the lines, thinking in compact code constructions, and joining and optimizing data exchange in new sequences, where, as a result, persons with a smartphone in their hands get access to a cosmic number of new impressions.

Now, we can all enroll for some courses, enter online universities, and order tens of books and manuals. We live in the melting pot of innovation history, and the lack of information is no excuse for the lack of talent. People began sharing their knowledge easily and understanding different questions, the answers to which are not worth publishing. Practical professional manuals are a separate, widely spread genre—littered, popular, and diverse.

This book appeared with the knowledge of similar books' faults. It was structured to be light but available, keeping the link to the authors' experiences and helping you to independently develop the basic principles of openFrameworks for any platform and projecting task. You will feel your personal evolution go on with every page, chapter, and every performed prototype.

We live in the epoch of Minecraft, when kids make worlds out of blocks and create the unimaginable, and the developers of this amazing game can consider themselves educators, teachers, and inspirers of an entire generation of future talents. We had no such games; we saw *The Prince of Persia*, who did his best jumping over the traps craftily set by the designers. We studied by less entire examples, but even then we realized that programming, coding, and UX impression design would be our new hobby, that not only spaceflights, but also the shimmering worlds of screens, internet services, new smart-stuffed objects, and the new economics of ideas is possible.

I have been teaching technology-based design for more than 10 years already; my main conclusion is that (the right) methods are neither simplification nor entertainment, which are characteristic of modern education. One should be inspired by what is achieved in the end and be captivated by the possibilities of the studied. Every elementary molecule of knowledge should be connected to a new use in one's imagination, excite an appetite for knowledge, and think in terms of practical application.

Thus, I got tens of projects made by graduate students, who had never been interested in programming at all. They came to love this creative process (though with hundreds of restrictions and only at the beginner level) because it allowed them to create their own companies and tens of commercial projects for clients.

A great couple—Processing and openFrameworks—permitted designers to create interactive systems, easily combining computer data and physical objects. They allowed creating interactive installations, thus widening the possibilities of device interfaces to experiment with data interpretation, transferring music into color, poetry into a drawing, and a dance into strokes of paint; to track down the behavior; to react; and to animate the behavior of digital nature inside an operating system and inside an application.

When I give my students a regular task without a basic introduction to technology or to some designers with no technical education, I just tell them to look around and think. This is because today there is no technology that wouldn't look like magic, or sorcery, as nudity looked profane but inspiring at the time of the Renaissance. This accessibility of naked technology in a book is not an anatomical atlas for openFrameworks but a collection of short, erotic stories inspiring to imagine, to make up and dream, and to try to master and capture with pleasure.

Probably, if the sexuality of programming were put in the first paragraph, my foreword would be read by more people. But to my mind, as a designer and a teacher, I care more about your turning the page over as this is where your personal border lies. There is the land separating the ocean of knowledge and experience from just a wish to know and understand. This feeling of border is the most mysterious thing in a person in his professional and personal evolution and in his personal creation. As Adam, we stand in front of the tree of knowledge. I envy you; you are students—beginners again.

Having read this book, I overstepped the professional line, allowing an insight into our projects in the near future and into understanding the logic and the principles of projecting with openFrameworks. Now, hold your breath and jump out of the ocean—turn the page!

Dmitry Karpov

Course Director, CPD Interactive Design and New Media, BHSAD

About the Authors

Denis Perevalov is a scientist at the Krasovsky Institute of Mathematics and Mechanics, Ekaterinburg, Russia. His main research interests are computer vision and interactive systems.

He has been teaching the information processing and algorithms of technical vision courses at the Ural Federal University since 2010. He is also the author of the book *Mastering openFrameworks – Creative Coding Demystified, Packt Publishing, 2013.*

I would like to thank my wife, Svetlana, and son, Timofey, for engaging me all the time.

Thanks to the Institute, especially my supervisor, Victor Borisovich Kostousov, for supporting my book writing.

Thanks to the dancer, Ekaterina Zharinova, for providing me with an opportunity to check the preliminary version of the book's video synthesizer in her media performance, *On the opposite side*.

I also give big thanks to Angelina Poptsova for proofreading, Oleg Nurmuhametov for consulting on iOS, and Ilya Nemihin from hackerspace (`makeitlab.ru`) for consulting on the Raspberry Pi.

Thanks to Packt Publishing for working so hard to make this book possible.

Many thanks to the openFrameworks creators and community for their constant enthusiasm and productivity.

Igor (Sodazot) Tatarnikov is a video artist, animator, and VJ from Moscow, Russia. He creates media content in various techniques, including animation, stop motion, and generative art.

Igor and Denis are cofounders of the visual laboratory Kuflex (2011), which made numerous interactive video installations and audio-visual performances for numerous exhibitions and commercial projects. Kuflex's clients include the Garage Museum of Contemporary Art (Moscow), the Jewish Museum and Tolerance Center (Moscow), the Moscow International Festival «Circle of light», Microsoft, Nokia, Samsung, and Master Card. Most of these works were made using openFrameworks.

I want to thank my wife, Marina, for her love and support; my parents for backing up all my interests since my childhood; and my jolly cat, Multick, for inspiration and good mood.

I would also like to thank Ksenya Lyashenko for interesting projects in our Kuflex team, Leksha Jankov for the music used in the book examples, and Kirill Ivanov for the visual experiments at SBPCH concerts and for the present that inspired the creation of the video synthesizer—the main example of the book.

My special thanks goes to the authors of openFrameworks and all the members of the community, who support its development, and also to Packt Publishing for working on the book.

About the Reviewers

Cory Barr is an interactive new media artist, data visualizer, and machine learning practitioner. A former machine-learning research scientist and engineer, he now focuses on the intersection of interactive installations and data visualization. He has a master's degree in computer science from Stanford University and a master's degree in music theory from the University of Oklahoma.

Cory has held positions at Stanford University, Genentech, and The Exploratorium. He is currently focused on Anticlockwise Arts, a company he cofounded to create interactive installations and data visualizations. His interactive art has been on display at cultural institutions and corporations, including The Exploratorium, California Academy of Sciences, The Tech Museum of Innovation, Audi, YouTube, and Yelp.

Dmitry Philonenko is a project leader, developer, designer, and an IT enthusiast with passion for innovations. He has been the Chief of Design since May 2007 in the development department at Animation Technologies Ltd. He has done his PhD (Cultural Studies / Critical Theory and Analysis) in the year 2008 from Ural State University, which is named after A.M. Gorky. He graduated from Ural State Academy of Architecture and Arts with a master's degree in graphic design (1997-2003).

Alex Samuel is a coder, maker, and a full-stack web developer who recently received her MFA, design and technology, from Parsons The New School For Design. Her work focuses on code-based interactions that encourage and augment the way people consume news. Currently, she is working to launch and develop Glossy.io with her cofounders.

Prior to entering the tech world, Alex worked as a beauty editor at Condé Nast for 5 years and continued to blog for `SELF.com` daily while in graduate school.

www.PacktPub.com

Support files, eBooks, discount offers, and more

For support files and downloads related to your book, please visit www.PacktPub.com.

Did you know that Packt offers eBook versions of every book published, with PDF and ePub files available? You can upgrade to the eBook version at www.PacktPub.com and as a print book customer, you are entitled to a discount on the eBook copy. Get in touch with us at service@packtpub.com for more details.

At www.PacktPub.com, you can also read a collection of free technical articles, sign up for a range of free newsletters and receive exclusive discounts and offers on Packt books and eBooks.

https://www2.packtpub.com/books/subscription/packtlib

Do you need instant solutions to your IT questions? PacktLib is Packt's online digital book library. Here, you can search, access, and read Packt's entire library of books.

Why subscribe?

- Fully searchable across every book published by Packt
- Copy and paste, print, and bookmark content
- On demand and accessible via a web browser

Free access for Packt account holders

If you have an account with Packt at www.PacktPub.com, you can use this to access PacktLib today and view 9 entirely free books. Simply use your login credentials for immediate access.

Table of Contents

Preface

openFrameworks Essentials is a guide that can be used to learn and use openFrameworks in order to develop creative and artistic real-time applications. The book contains an insight into how openFrameworks can be used to implement your creative ideas in powerful projects by working on the OS X, Windows, Linux, iOS, Android, and Raspberry Pi devices. Although openFrameworks is a very popular toolkit for creative coding, the number of books describing openFrameworks is not high.

This book is a fast-paced tutorial that begins with installing openFrameworks and then takes a step-by-step approach towards using openFrameworks to build a video synthesizer project. We will investigate and implement features such as 2D and 3D graphics, GUI, shaders, and reaction on sound, using the OSC networking protocol and Arduino.

The openFrameworks version considered is 0.8.4.

What this book covers

Chapter 1, Getting Started with openFrameworks, introduces openFrameworks by explaining its installation and running one of its examples. Additionally, it discusses the structure of the video synthesizer project, which will be developed in the course of the book.

Chapter 2, Creating Your First openFrameworks Project, guides you to create a new openFrameworks project and implement 2D graphics.

Chapter 3, Adding a GUI and Handling Keyboard Events, explains creating a graphical user interface consisting of controls such as sliders and checkboxes. Also, it covers implementing keyboard events, using system dialogs, and saving screenshots.

Chapter 4, Working with Raster Graphics – Images, Videos, and Shaders, explains drawing images and videos, capturing video from a camera, mixing videos using additive blending, and creating the *kaleidoscope* video effect using a fragment shader.

Chapter 5, Creating 3D Graphics, introduces the basics of 3D graphics with openFrameworks by drawing a sphere in 3D and then texturing and deforming it.

Chapter 6, Animating Parameters, discusses using various data sources, such as Perlin noise, sounds, and text files, to automatically control the parameters of the project.

Chapter 7, Distributed and Physical Computing with Networking and Arduino, explains how to control your project from other programs using the OSC networking protocol. It describes building such controlling programs using openFrameworks by itself as well as the Python and Max/MSP programming languages. Also, it covers receiving data from an Arduino device.

Chapter 8, Deploying the Project on iOS, Android, and Raspberry Pi, guides you to run the light version of the developed video synthesizer on mobile and Raspberry Pi devices.

Chapter 9, Further Resources, suggests the direction to further enhance the video synthesizer project, provides sources of additional information on openFrameworks, and discusses debugging and speeding up openFrameworks projects.

Appendix A, Video Synthesizer Reference, is a comprehensive documentation of the developed video synthesizer project. It contains a description of all GUI controls, control keys, and media files used by the project.

Appendix B, openFrameworks Quick Reference, is a useful reminder of the basic openFrameworks functions and classes used in the book.

What you need for this book

openFrameworks is a cross-platform toolkit, so you can develop openFrameworks projects using your operating system of choice—OS X, Windows, Linux Ubuntu, Debian or Fedora, or Raspbian OS. To build the projects, you will need to install the C++ IDE and openFrameworks itself. All the required software is free; detailed instructions on installing are explained in *Chapter 1, Getting Started with openFrameworks*.

To proceed with some sections, you will need additional software (Python and Max/MSP) or hardware (camera, microphone, iOS, Android, Raspberry Pi, and Arduino devices). If you currently don't have any devices, you can skip the corresponding section(s).

Who this book is for

The book is intended for those who want to use openFrameworks to build creative projects that run at maximum efficiency on desktops and mobiles. Perhaps you have some experience in creative coding but have never used C++ and openFrameworks, or perhaps you know a little C++ but are new to creative coding. In either case, this book will get you up and running quickly. A basic knowledge of programming languages, such as C++, Java, Python, or JavaScript, will be enough to proceed with the book.

Conventions

In this book, you will find a number of text styles that distinguish between different kinds of information. Here are some examples of these styles and an explanation of their meaning.

Code words in text, database table names, folder names, filenames, file extensions, pathnames, dummy URLs, user input, and Twitter handles are shown as follows: "The class for playing videos is `ofVideoPlayer`."

A block of code is set as follows:

```
ofSetWindowTitle( "Video synth" );
ofSetWindowShape( 1280, 720 );
ofSetFrameRate( 60 );
ofBackground( ofColor::white );
```

When we wish to draw your attention to a particular part of a code block, the relevant lines or items are set in bold:

```
for (int i=-50; i<50; i++) {
  ofPushMatrix();
  ofTranslate( i*20, 0 );
  ofLine( 0, -100, 0, 100 );
  ofPopMatrix();
}
```

Any command-line input or output is written as follows:

```
cd openFrameworks/libs/openFrameworksCompiled/project
```

New terms and **important words** are shown in bold. Words that you see on the screen, for example, in menus or dialog boxes, appear in the text like this: "Click on the **GENERATE PROJECT** button."

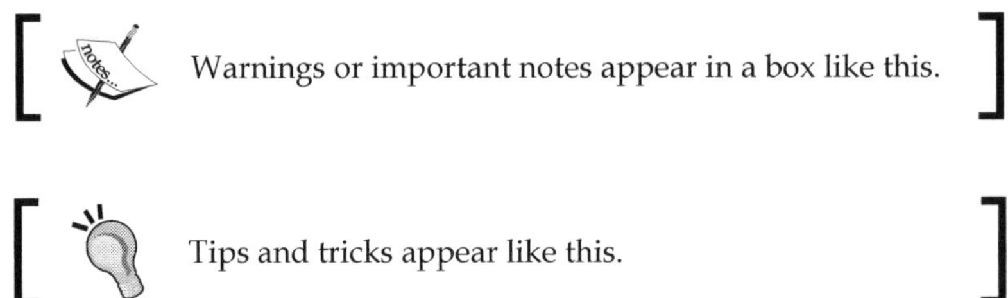

[Warnings or important notes appear in a box like this.]

[Tips and tricks appear like this.]

Reader feedback

Feedback from our readers is always welcome. Let us know what you think about this book—what you liked or disliked. Reader feedback is important for us as it helps us develop titles that you will really get the most out of.

To send us general feedback, simply e-mail `feedback@packtpub.com`, and mention the book's title in the subject of your message.

If there is a topic that you have expertise in and you are interested in either writing or contributing to a book, see our author guide at `www.packtpub.com/authors`.

Customer support

Now that you are the proud owner of a Packt book, we have a number of things to help you to get the most from your purchase.

Downloading the example code

You can download the example code files from your account at `http://www.packtpub.com` for all the Packt Publishing books you have purchased. If you purchased this book elsewhere, you can visit `http://www.packtpub.com/support` and register to have the files e-mailed directly to you.

Downloading the color images of this book

We also provide you with a PDF file that has color images of the screenshots/diagrams used in this book. The color images will help you better understand the changes in the output. You can download this file from: `https://www.packtpub.com/sites/default/files/downloads/61450S_Graphics.pdf`.

Errata

Although we have taken every care to ensure the accuracy of our content, mistakes do happen. If you find a mistake in one of our books—maybe a mistake in the text or the code—we would be grateful if you could report this to us. By doing so, you can save other readers from frustration and help us improve subsequent versions of this book. If you find any errata, please report them by visiting `http://www.packtpub.com/submit-errata`, selecting your book, clicking on the **Errata Submission Form** link, and entering the details of your errata. Once your errata are verified, your submission will be accepted and the errata will be uploaded to our website or added to any list of existing errata under the Errata section of that title.

To view the previously submitted errata, go to `https://www.packtpub.com/books/content/support` and enter the name of the book in the search field. The required information will appear under the **Errata** section.

Piracy

Piracy of copyrighted material on the Internet is an ongoing problem across all media. At Packt, we take the protection of our copyright and licenses very seriously. If you come across any illegal copies of our works in any form on the Internet, please provide us with the location address or website name immediately so that we can pursue a remedy.

Please contact us at `copyright@packtpub.com` with a link to the suspected pirated material.

We appreciate your help in protecting our authors and our ability to bring you valuable content.

Questions

If you have a problem with any aspect of this book, you can contact us at `questions@packtpub.com`, and we will do our best to address the problem.

1
Getting Started with openFrameworks

In this chapter, we will introduce openFrameworks by covering the following topics:

- What is openFrameworks?
- Installing openFrameworks
- Running an openFrameworks example

Finally, we will discuss the video synthesizer project, which we will develop throughout the book.

What is openFrameworks?

openFrameworks is a free, open source C++ framework that is intended to develop real-time projects, which use most modern computing devices' capabilities, such as video, audio, networking, and computer vision.

openFrameworks is developed by Zach Lieberman, Theodore Watson, and Arturo Castro, together with a big openFrameworks community. The current openFrameworks version is 0.8.4.

Its main features are:

- openFrameworks is a framework for the easy development of real-time applications. All you need to do is implement a number of events, such as *starting project* and *drawing*, and openFrameworks will maintain all the stuff behind this, such as creating a graphical window and listening for mouse and keyboard events.

- Its conception and philosophy is oriented for use in creative and experimental projects. openFrameworks contain many ready-to-use functions and classes to work with 2D and 3D graphics, video, audio, and so on.
- It's a C++ framework, that is, you will code it using the C++ programming language. Your code will be compiled in native machine code and executed very efficiently. Many algorithms that work slowly when implemented in languages such as Python, Java, or Processing, could work significantly faster when implemented in openFrameworks.
- openFrameworks is highly extensible. Its extensions are called **addons**. They are open source and are built by members of the openFrameworks community. Several hundreds of existing addons give you an opportunity to extend your project with the capabilities of various software libraries, popular sensors, and gadgets.
- openFrameworks is **cross-platform** — the code you will write can be executed on many popular platforms, including OS X, Windows, Linux, iOS, Android, and Linux ARM devices such as Raspberry Pi.
- Finally, it has a very friendly and active community. If you get stuck during developing with openFrameworks, you can get help from the openFrameworks forum.

Begin your acquaintance with openFrameworks by visiting and exploring its site `openframeworks.cc`. It contains a lot of useful information about openFrameworks, including download links, tutorials, documentation, forums, and news.

Installing openFrameworks

To develop projects with openFrameworks, you need to install an **Integrated Development Environment** (**IDE**) with the C++ compiler and openFrameworks.

To install them, perform the following steps:

1. Go to openFrameworks' download page at `openframeworks.cc/download`.
2. Find your platform on the page (OS X, Linux, Windows, iOS, Android, or Linux ARM) and select the desired IDE (Xcode, Code::Blocks, Eclipse, or Visual Studio). For developing with iOS, an OS X computer is required. Development on a Linux ARM device is done using the C++ compiler directly, without an IDE.

All the IDEs mentioned are free. But, to run your project on an iOS device, you must buy an iOS Developer License from Apple for $99 per year.

3. Download the openFrameworks archive by clicking on the corresponding link and unzip it.
4. Click on the corresponding setup guide link and follow the instructions shown for installing and configuring the IDE and openFrameworks. Now you can develop and run your projects in openFrameworks.

> Running openFrameworks projects on desktops (Mac OS X, Windows, or Linux) is simpler than on mobiles. So, if you are a novice in C++ or openFrameworks, we recommend that you start to develop your very first openFrameworks project for a desktop OS rather than a mobile one.
>
> After a while, when you are a little more comfortable with C++ and openFrameworks, you can easily port your project to mobiles, if needed. You will learn how to deploy openFrameworks projects on mobiles and Raspberry Pi in *Chapter 8, Deploying the Project on iOS, Android, and Raspberry Pi*.

The openFrameworks folder structure

It's time to look inside openFrameworks, so open the openFrameworks folder. It consists of a number of folders and files, as shown in the following screenshot (the screenshot is for OS X, but the folder structure is similar for all other platforms):

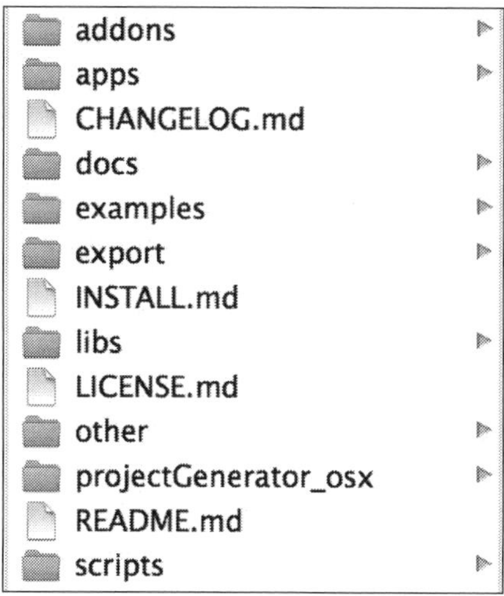

openFrameworks' folder structure

The most important folders for us now are `apps` and `examples`. The `apps` folder is the place where your own projects will be stored. The `examples` folder contains a collection of examples, demonstrating all the aspects of openFrameworks programming. The examples are categorized by topics, including 3D, graphics, sound, and video.

Now, let's run one of the examples.

Running your first example

We would like to introduce one of the funniest openFrameworks examples, which we like a lot. The example captures the images from a webcam and draws it on the screen as a fancy 3D surface, as shown in the following picture:

3D surface generated by an openFrameworks example

This is the `meshFromCamera` example located in the `examples/3d` folder.

> This example requires a webcam. If your computer does not have a built-in webcam, and you have no external webcam to connect to, please work with another example, for instance, `examples/3d/3DPrimitivesExample`.

We cannot run the example immediately after installing openFrameworks. The reason is that openFrameworks examples are distributed as source files only, without executable files that you can run.

To obtain the executable file, we need to build the project, that is, compile its C++ source code to machine code and link it into an executable file. Let's do it and then run the example by performing the following steps:

1. Open the example folder `examples/3d/meshFromCamera`.
2. Find there the file named `meshFromCamera.xcodeproj` (Xcode project), `meshFromCamera.sln` (Visual Studio project), or `meshFromCamera.workspace` (Code::Blocks project).
3. Double-click on this file, and the `meshFromCamera` project will open in your IDE.
4. Build the project by pressing *Command* + *B* in Xcode, *F7* in Visual Studio, or by clicking on the **Build** button in Code::Blocks.

For Xcode users

In the project, there exist several schemes that indicate the part of the project to build and a number of settings for it. Often at first run, the scheme is set to **openFrameworks**, as shown on the following screenshot:

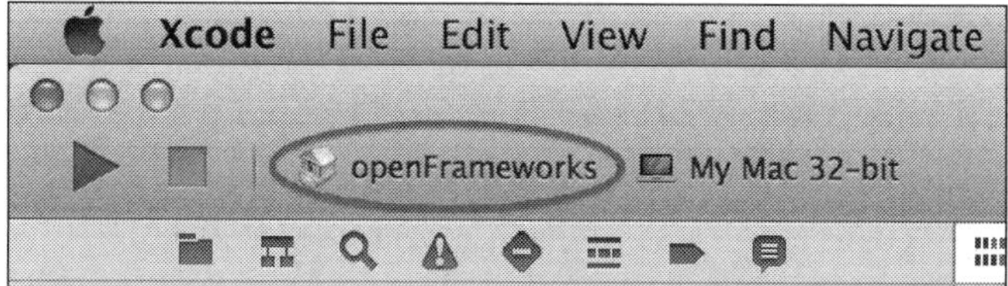

Scheme selector in Xcode

If so, the compiler builds openFrameworks, but not the project. To resolve the issue, please click on the scheme name. A context menu will appear. Select the **meshFromCamera Release** scheme there. After this, perform building as described in step 4.

5. Run the project by clicking on the corresponding button in your IDE (normally, it's depicted as a small triangle, meaning the play symbol). After running, you will see your webcam's image drawn as a distorted 3D surface.
6. Press *Esc* to stop the execution.

This example involves several topics, such as capturing frames from the camera, creating 3D surfaces, and texturing them. You will discover these topics in *Chapter 4, Working with Raster Graphics – Images, Videos, and Shaders*, and *Chapter 5, Creating 3D Graphics*, and will be able to build similar and even more sophisticated projects easily.

The video synthesizer application

A **video synthesizer** is an electronic device or a computer program that generates and transforms a video signal in a complex way. Video synthesizers are used for creating live visuals for DJ sets and performances, or serve as a visual part of interactive installations and mobile apps.

Probably the most famous analog video synthesizer was made by John Whitney in the middle of the twentieth century. Visual effects, obtained with the synthesizer, are demonstrated in his film *Catalog* (1961). It's worth watching on YouTube.

Throughout the book, we will build our own video synthesizer application. We will start with a simple project in the next chapter and will extend it by adding new features with each new chapter. At the end of the book, we will get a fully-fledged video synthesizer, which reveals many openFrameworks capabilities.

Typically, a video synthesizer consists of several modules—video generators, video players, video effects, and video mixers—connected to each other. Our synthesizer will include all these basic modules and will have the following structure:

- A 2D image generator that produces pictures made from geometric shapes, (*Chapter 2, Creating Your First openFrameworks Project*)
- A **graphical user interface** (**GUI**) consisting of sliders and checkboxes (*Chapter 3, Adding a GUI and Handling Keyboard Events*)
- A player of image files, video files, and live videos from a camera (*Chapter 4, Working with Raster Graphics – Images, Videos, and Shaders*)
- A video mixer that mixes several pictures using additive blending and the kaleidoscope video effect (*Chapter 4, Working with Raster Graphics – Images, Videos, and Shaders*)
- A 3D surface generator that renders a textured and deformed sphere in 3D (*Chapter 5, Creating 3D Graphics*)

- Various sources for controlling the synthesizer's parameters, such as LFO, sound analysis, text files (*Chapter 6, Animating Parameters*), networking, and an Arduino device (*Chapter 7, Distributed and Physical Computing with Networking and Arduino*)

This structure is shown in the following diagram:

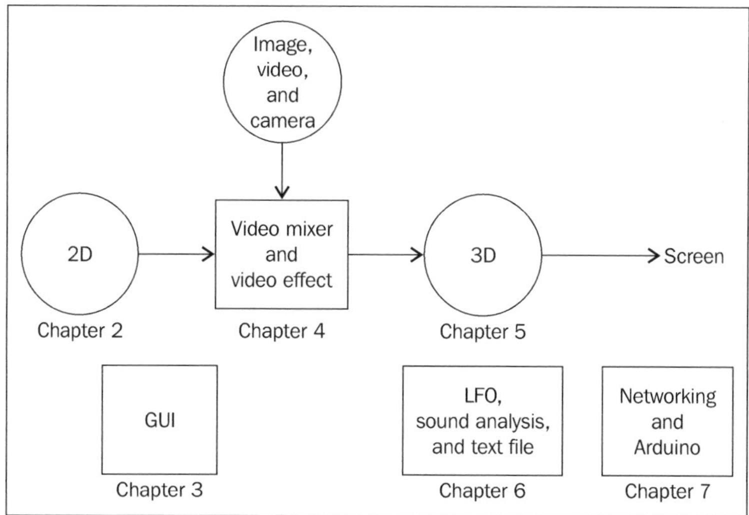

The video synthesizer's structure

Additionally, in *Chapter 8, Deploying the Project on iOS, Android, and Raspberry Pi*, we will see how to deploy the light version of the synthesizer on mobile devices: iOS, Android, and Raspberry Pi. In the last chapter, *Chapter 9, Further Resources*, we will consider ways to further enhance the synthesizer, get some advice on debugging and optimizing your future openFrameworks projects, and consider additional references on openFrameworks.

The synthesizer created will have quite a lot of GUI controls and control keys. If while working with the book you need a quick reference on some of them, please see *Appendix A, Video Synthesizer Reference*, where we have collected descriptions and references to all parts of the synthesizer.

For a short description of openFrameworks functions and classes discussed throughout the book, see *Appendix B, openFrameworks Quick Reference*.

Three reasons to create your own video synthesizer with openFrameworks

Why would you program a video synthesizer with openFrameworks? The reasons are the following:

- You will get a handy, standalone application that provides you with interactive video wherever you need it (on a stage at your live performance or in your mobile), running on any platforms, and controlled by other programs or devices, such as mobiles or Arduino.
- Our video synthesizer is exceptionally customizable. By changing just several lines of code, you will get a unique synthesizer. The more you change the code, the more you find that there are no limits to expressing your creative ideas.
- By splitting the video synthesizer project into parts and then rearranging and adding new parts, you will obtain something different from the video synthesizer. For example, you can construct an interactive installation that transforms users' faces into abstract images. It could even be a mobile 3D drawing application that generates fantastic 3D landscapes. It's worth noting that you can easily incorporate LeapMotion, Kinect, and many other gadgets into your openFrameworks project in order to realize the interactive experience that you want.

Summary

In this chapter, you learned what openFrameworks is, how to install it, and also how to build and run its examples.

In the next chapter, we will create our own openFrameworks project that draws simple 2D graphics.

2
Creating Your First openFrameworks Project

In the previous chapter, we installed openFrameworks and learned how to build and run its example projects. It's time to start our own project! So, in this chapter, we are going to develop a sketch of the video synthesizer and explore the basics of 2D graphics with openFrameworks.

We will cover the following topics:

- Creating a new project with Project Generator
- openFrameworks project's structure
- Setting up screen size and frame rate
- Drawing geometric primitives, such as lines, triangles, and circles
- Drawing patterns from geometric primitives

Creating and running a new project

Let's create a new openFrameworks project. The simplest way to do this is to use the **Project Generator** wizard included in openFrameworks for OS X, Windows, Linux, and iOS.

> Another way to create a new project is to copy any openFrameworks example to the `apps/myApps` folder (or any other subfolder of the `apps` folder) and use it from scratch for your project. The first thing you would need to do after copying is rename the project; please see the documentation of your IDE for details on how to do this.

Creating a project

To create a project, follow these steps:

1. **Run Project Generator** : Open the `ProjectGenerator_osx` folder (in OS X), `ProjectGenerator` (in Windows), or `apps/projectGenerator` (in Linux) and run the executable named `projectGenerator`.

[In Linux, Project Generator needs to be built before running; see the details on building a project in the *Running your first example* section of *Chapter 1, Getting Started with openFrameworks*.]

You will see the Project Generator window, as shown in the following screenshot:

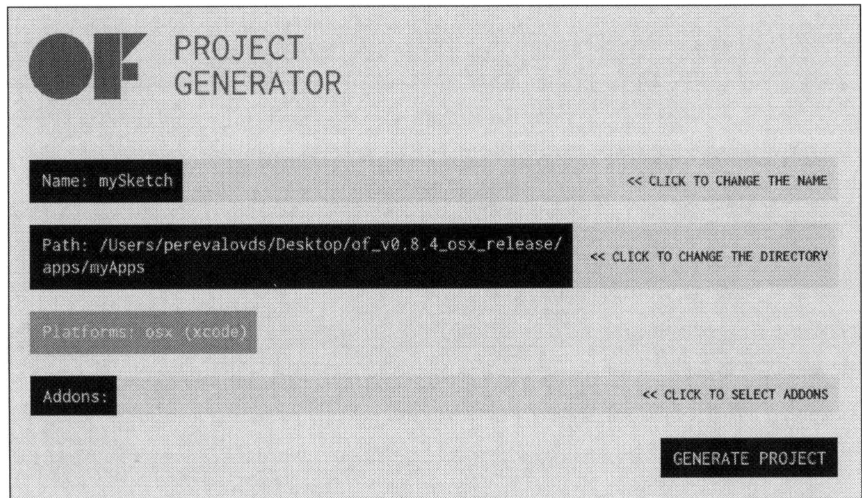

This is the Project Generator window

2. **Set project name**: Click on the area titled **Name: mySketch**. The dialog prompting a name for your project will appear. Type `VideoSynth` and click on the **OK** button to close the dialog.

[In the name of the project, you cannot use non-ASCII symbols. Also, note that spaces will be replaced by _.]

3. **Choosing the project's path**: By default, your project will be created in the `apps/myApps` folder. If you want to change the destination folder, click on the area titled **Path:...**.

> You must put your openFrameworks project inside some subfolder of the `apps` folder (more precisely, your project must be placed at a *third* level, away from the root of the openFrameworks folder). Otherwise, you will get a compile error because the compiler didn't find openFrameworks files. For instance, `apps/myApps` and `apps/BigProject` folders are appropriate folders for your openFrameworks projects.

4. **Selecting the addons**: Addons are openFrameworks extensions. The most important addons are distributed with openFrameworks (these addons are called **core addons**). All other addons are called **non-core addons** and are listed on `ofxaddons.com`. They should be downloaded and installed manually to the `addons` folder of openFrameworks.

   In our project, we will use two core addons—`ofxGui` and `ofxOsc`. These addons implement GUI and networking via the **Open Sound Control** (**OSC**) protocol. We will discuss them in detail later in *Chapter 3, Adding a GUI and Handling Keyboard Events*, and *Chapter 7, Distributed and Physical Computing with Networking and Arduino*.

   To link them to the project, click on the area titled **Addons:**. The dialog with the installed addons list will appear. Check the **ofxGui** and **ofxOsc** checkboxes and click on the **<< BACK** button.

5. Now, the Project Generator window should look as shown in the following screenshot:

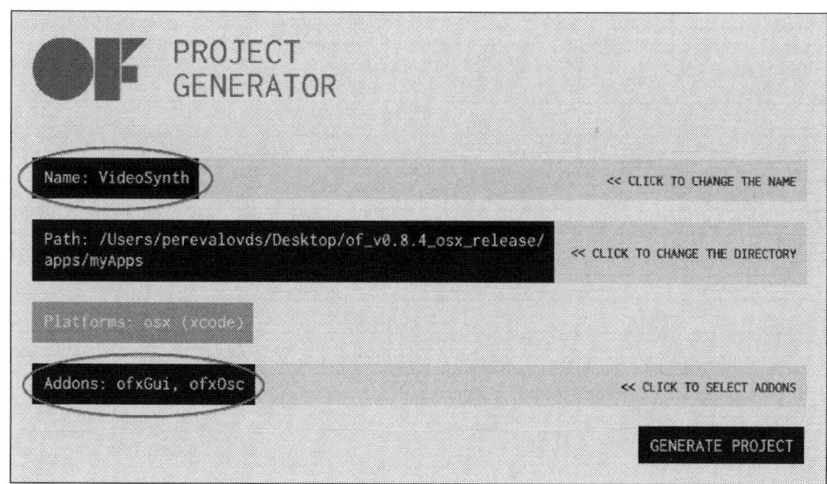

Here, Project Generator is ready to create our video synthesizer project

Make sure that **Name:** is set to **VideoSynth**, and **Addons:** is set to **ofxGui, ofxOsc**.

6. Click on the **GENERATE PROJECT** button. The `VideoSynth` project will be created.
7. Close the Project Generator application by pressing *Esc*.

Running a project

Now, let's run our project with the following steps:

1. Open the `apps/myApps/VideoSynth` project in your IDE.
2. Build and run it (see the *Running your first example* section of *Chapter 1, Getting Started with openFrameworks*). You will see the project's window, as shown in the following screenshot:

This is the window of the new project created by Project Generator

3. Press *Esc* to close the application.

Great! We have a project that builds and runs. Currently, it shows a blank window and does nothing interesting. So, in the rest of the chapter, we will fill it with meaningful code. Before we do it, let's discover the project's structure to know exactly the places where we should add the code.

Discovering the project's code structure

Open the project's `VideoSynth` folder and find the `src` folder there. It contains the project's source code files, as shown in the following screenshot:

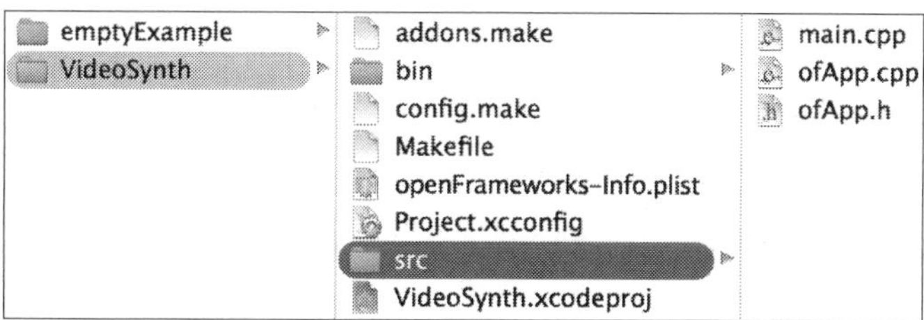

The project's folder contents (the center column) and its source code files placed in the src folder (the right column)

There are three source files:

- `main.cpp`: This file contains the code to initiate a window and run the app. We will leave it unchanged.
- `ofApp.h`: This file is a declaration of the `ofApp` application class, which consists of a declaration of the functions, such as `setup()`, `update()`, `draw()`, and some others. Currently, we do not need to add anything there.
- `ofApp.cpp`: This file contains definitions of declared functions. This is the file we will edit right now.

The following functions, declared in the `ofApp` class, are called by the openFrameworks engine:

- `setup()`: This function is called once at the beginning of the application execution. This is the place to implement a project's initialization steps, such as loading images, starting cameras, and initializing networking.
- `update()`: This is called after `setup()`, and this is the place to perform computations and related things, such as camera updating and network receiving and sending.
- `draw()`: This is called after `update()`. All that needs to be drawn on the screen should be coded here. After a while, depending on the frame rate settings, openFrameworks calls `update()` and `draw()` again and again, in an infinite loop.
- `exit()`: This is called right before finishing the application execution. This is the final step of the program. Here, you should stop all the started processes, such as cameras and networking.

- All the other functions currently presented in the class declaration are called by openFrameworks to handle various events, including keyboard keys pressed (`keyPressed()`), mouse clicks (`mousePressed()`), and changing window size (`windowResized()`).

Setting up the screen

The very first thing to code is to set up the global attributes: the project's window title, screen size, rendering frame rate, and background color. To achieve this, add the following lines to the `ofApp::setup()` function's body in the `ofApp.cpp` file:

```
ofSetWindowTitle( "Video synth" );
ofSetWindowShape( 1280, 720 );
ofSetFrameRate( 60 );
ofBackground( ofColor::white );
```

Downloading the example code

You can download the example code files from your account at `http://www.packtpub.com` for all the Packt Publishing books you have purchased. If you purchased this book elsewhere, you can visit `http://www.packtpub.com/support` and register to have the files e-mailed directly to you.

This code consists of calling four openFrameworks functions, which set the window title to **Video synth**, the project's drawing area size with width of `1280` pixels and height of `720` pixels, the frame rate to `60` Hz, and the white background, respectively.

All openFrameworks functions and class names begin with **of**, which is an abbreviation of **openFrameworks**.

Run the project and you will see a titled window with a white background:

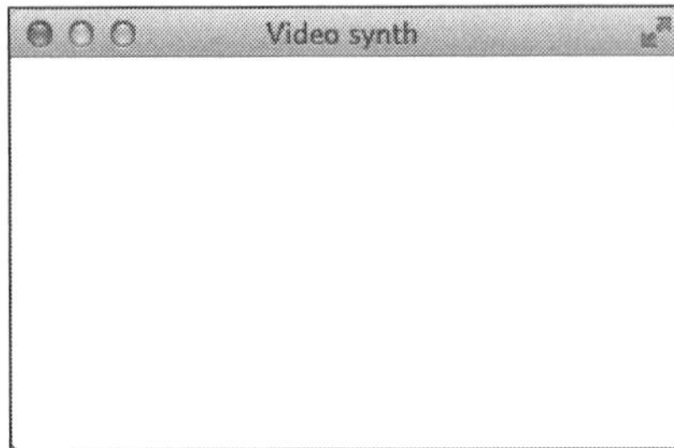

This shows the project's window with a title and a white background

By default, the project runs in the windowed mode. To set the fullscreen mode, add the following line:

```
ofSetFullscreen( true );
```

The `true` argument here means that you are enabling fullscreen.

Centering the coordinate system

By default, in openFrameworks (and in most computer programs dealing with 2D graphics), the center of the screen coordinate system is placed in the top-left corner of the screen. The horizontal axis is directed to the right and the vertical axis is directed downwards. The measurement unit is the pixel.

For a screen with size 1280 × 720 pixels, the top-left corner has the coordinates **(0, 0)** and the bottom-right corner has the coordinates (1280-1, 720-1) = **(1279, 719)**, as shown in the following screenshot:

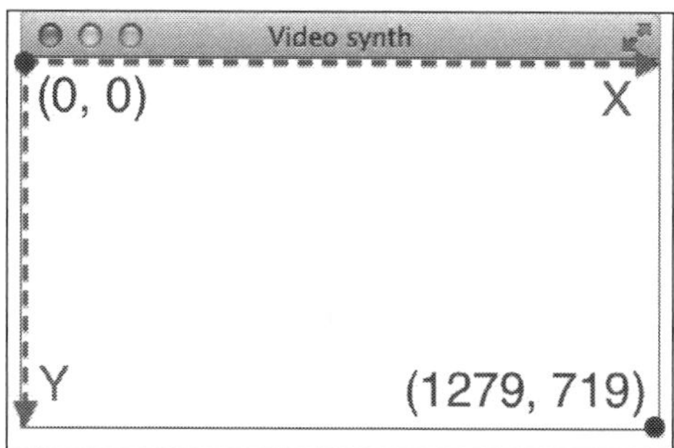

This shows the default coordinate system

We are planning to implement generative graphics, which is situated around the screen center. To make the code easier, it's a good approach to move the coordinate system origin to the screen center by adding the following lines to the `ofApp::draw()` function:

```
ofPushMatrix();
ofTranslate( ofGetWidth() / 2, ofGetHeight() / 2 );
//----
//...       We will place our drawing code here
//----
ofPopMatrix();
```

The `ofPushMatrix()` function pushes the current coordinate system state (represented by a *view matrix*) in a special stack that holds view matrices. Then, the `ofTranslate()` command shifts the coordinate system by `ofGetWidth()/2` pixels horizontally and `ofGetHeight()/2` pixels vertically. The `ofGetWidth()` and `ofGetHeight()` functions return the current screen size, so we obtain a shift of the coordinate system center to the screen center. The `//...` comment line defines the place where we will put the drawing code a bit later. Finally, the `ofPopMatrix()` calling restores the original coordinate system by getting it from the stack.

We obtain the centered coordinate system, as shown in the following screenshot:

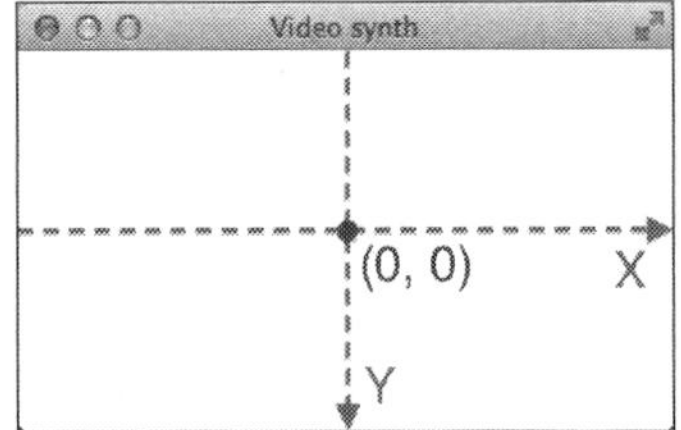

This shows the centered coordinate system

We are ready to drop some graphics on the screen!

A simple drawing

The simplest thing that can be drawn with openFrameworks is a geometric primitive such as a line, rectangle, or circle. Before drawing, we should set the drawing color using the `ofSetColor` function and then draw primitives using commands such as `ofLine`, `ofRect`, `ofTriangle`, and `ofCircle` (they draw a line, rectangle, triangle, and circle respectively). Let's consider setting the color and then drawing functions in detail.

Setting drawing color

The `ofSetColor` function switches the drawing color to a specified color. There are several overloaded versions of this function:

- The most universal form lets us explicitly specify the red, green, blue, and alpha (opaqueness) components of the color:

  ```
  ofSetColor( 255, 0, 0, 255 );
  ```

  The arguments are integers from 0 to 255, which correspond to red, green, or blue color components and alpha color components. In our example, we will get the red opaque color because the red component is maximal, the blue and green components are zero, and the opaqueness is maximal.

- When the fourth argument is omitted, it means alpha=255, so to obtain the red color, we could use the shorter command, as shown in the following line of code:

  ```
  ofSetColor( 255, 0, 0 );
  ```

- If only one argument is given, it means an opaque color with specified brightness, as shown in the following line of code:

  ```
  ofSetColor( 128 );
  ```

  This command is equivalent to calling `ofSetColor(128, 128, 128, 255);` and getting a gray opaque color.

- Also, it is possible to specify the color's name, as follows:

  ```
  ofSetColor( ofColor::yellow );
  ```

  This command sets a yellow drawing color.

The list of all available color names is given in the `ofColors.h` file in openFrameworks.

- When you need to set the same color several times or want to pass it as an argument to a function, you could use the `ofColor` class:

  ```
  ofColor color( 255, 0, 0 );
  ofSetColor( color );
  ```

  This code creates a `color` variable that holds the red color and then uses it to set a drawing color.

By default, openFrameworks uses a white color to draw. But, we also use a white color for the background. Hence, to be able to see our drawing, we must set a drawing color different than white, for example, black. To achieve this, add the following command to the `ofApp::draw()` function between two comments `//----`:

```
ofSetColor( ofColor::black );
```

Drawing primitives

We collected the most important primitives' drawing functions and some additional functions in the following table. It contains a function's description, its example code, and its resulting diagram:

Function and description	Code example	Result
`ofLine(x1, y1, x2, y2)` This draws a straight line segment from (x1,y1) to (x2,y2).	`ofLine( 0, -100, 0, 100 );` `//A line`	

`ofSetLineWidth( w )`
This sets the width of drawing lines.
	`ofSetLineWidth( 3.0 );`
	`ofLine( 0, -100, 0, 100 );`
	`//A thick line`	

`ofRect( x, y, w, h )` This draws a rectangle with the top-left corner (x, y), width w, and height h pixels.	`ofRect( 0, 0, 100, 50 );` `//A rectangle`	
`ofTriangle(x1,y1, x2,y2,x3,y3)` This draws a triangle with vertices (x1,y1), (x2, y2), (x3, y3).	`ofTriangle(0,0,-50,100,50,100);` `//A triangle`	
`ofCircle( x, y, r )` This draws a circle with center at (x,y) and radius r.	`ofCircle( 0, 0, 50 );` `//A circle`	
`ofSetCircleResolution(q)` The circle's boundary is drawn as a equilateral polygon. This function sets the number of vertices for the polygon. The default value is 20.	`ofSetCircleResolution(40);` `//A smoother circle`	

Function and description	Code example	Result

`ofFill()`
 	
This enables the filling of drawn shapes (it is enabled by default).
	`ofFill();`
	`ofRect( 0, 0, 100, 50 );`
	//Filled rectangle	

`ofNoFill()`
 	
This disables the filling of drawn shapes.
	`ofNoFill();`
	`ofRect( 0, 0, 100, 50 );`
	//Unfilled rectangle	

All coordinates and parameters in the drawing functions are floats, except the argument of the `ofSetCircleResolution` command, which should be an integer.

To check any of these code examples, insert it after the `ofSetColor...` line.

If you have never programmed such drawings, you can stop reading for the moment and explore drawing simple pictures from the listed primitives, using different colors!

Now, let's go further and explore a way of creating pictures by repeatedly drawing the same primitive.

Before moving to the next section, please comment (or remove) the code you created in this section when drawing primitives so that the `draw()` function looks as follows:

```
ofPushMatrix();
ofTranslate( ofGetWidth() / 2, ofGetHeight() / 2 );
//----

//----
ofPopMatrix();
```

Geometric patterns

The idea of creating a picture by repeatedly drawing several geometric primitives and shifting, rotating, or resizing them in small amounts is known from ancient times. The resultant picture is called a **geometric pattern**.

Ethnic ornaments are exciting examples of geometric patterns. Check Google's image search results on the *geometric pattern* and *ethnic ornament* to boost your creativity on the topic.

Creating geometric patterns with a computer is super easy, and it's a must-have feature of any video synthesizer. In the rest of the chapter, we will implement a simple but powerful pattern's type in detail, which we call a **stripe pattern**.

The stripe pattern

A **stripe pattern** is formed by drawing the geometric primitives repeatedly, placing their centers along some (invisible) curve, such as a straight line, a curved line, or even a spiral. We will call this curve a **base curve**.

The reason of naming is that the resultant figure sometimes resembles a stripe.

A stripe pattern made from parallel lines

Let's draw a pattern that has a horizontal straight line as a base curve and a vertical line segment as a geometric primitive, as shown in the following image:

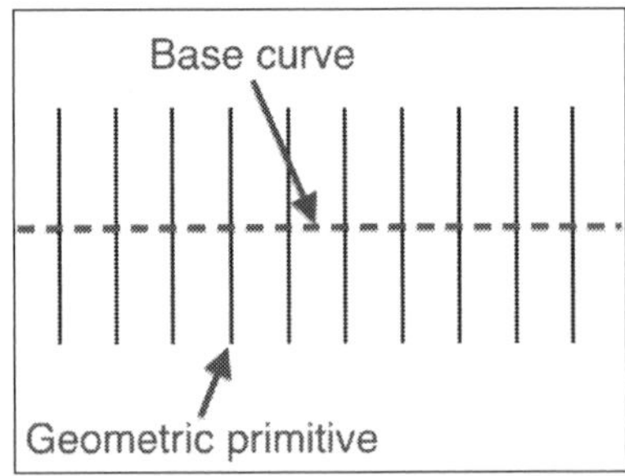

This shows a simple stripe pattern scheme

For convenience, we will implement the pattern drawing as a new function called `stripePattern()`. The implementation will consist of three steps: inserting the function declaration, function definition, and calling this function from the `draw()` function.

Inserting the function declaration

Insert the following line of our function declaration to the `ofApp.h` file, as follows:

```
void stripePattern();
```

This line must be placed inside the `ofApp` class declaration, somewhere after the `public:` keyword line. The exact position of the line is not important. The resulting code can look like the following:

```
class ofApp : public ofBaseApp{
public:
  void setup();
  void update();
  void draw();
  void stripePattern();
```

Inserting the function definition

Insert the following code (for instance, insert it before the `ofApp::draw()` function definition) to the `ofApp.cpp` file:

```
void ofApp::stripePattern() {
  ofSetColor( ofColor::black );
  ofSetLineWidth( 3.0 );
  for (int i=-50; i<50; i++) {
    ofPushMatrix();
    ofTranslate( i*20, 0 );
    ofLine( 0, -100, 0, 100 );
    ofPopMatrix();
  }
}
```

The first two lines of the function set the drawing color to black and the drawing line's width to `3` pixels (we discussed these functions in the preceding section). The third line starts a `for` cycle, which iterates `i` from `-50` to `49`.

The cycle's body consists of storing the current coordinate system, shifting it by `( i*20, 0 )`, drawing a vertical line, and restoring the coordinate system back to the original state.

As you would note, the cycle will produce the following sequence of coordinate system centers:

*(-50*20, 0), (-49*20, 0), …, (0, 0), (20, 0), …, (49*20, 0)*

These points lie on the horizontal line $y = 0$— this is the equation for the base curve of the pattern. By drawing vertical lines in each iteration, we obtain the desired pattern.

The `stripePattern()` function is ready. Let's call it.

Inserting the function calling

Insert the `stripePattern();` code line into the `ofApp::draw()` function between the two comments `//----`. The `ofApp::draw()` function should now look like this:

```
ofPushMatrix();
ofTranslate( ofGetWidth() / 2, ofGetHeight() / 2 );
//----
stripePattern();
//----
ofPopMatrix();
```

On running the project, we will see the desired pattern, as shown in the following image:

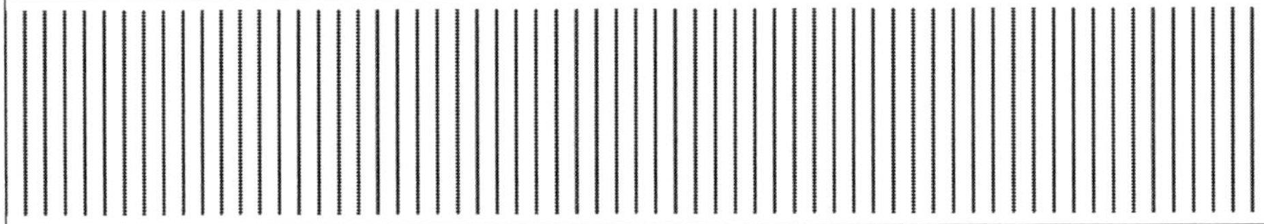

Here's a stripe pattern made from parallel lines

A stripe pattern made from rotating lines

Let's improve the pattern generation algorithm by adding a rotation of lines. Insert the following line before the `ofLine...` command inside `ofApp::stripePattern()`:

```
ofRotate( i * 5 );
```

This command rotates the coordinate system by `i * 5` degrees counterclockwise. It results in the following pattern:

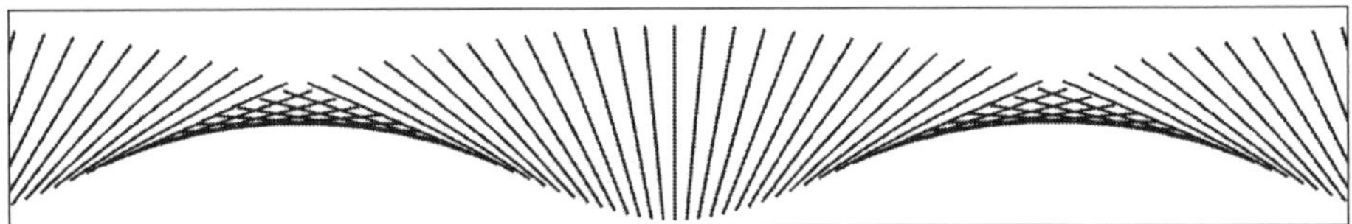

This is a stripe pattern made from rotating lines

A stripe pattern made from rotating triangles

Until now, our pattern really looks like a stripe. But, this is not the case always. To demonstrate this, let's draw a big triangle instead of a line. Replace the `ofLine...` line inside the `stripePattern()` function with the following lines:

```
ofScale( 6, 6 );
ofTriangle( 0, 0, -50, 100, 50, 100 );
```

The first line scales the coordinate system six fold, so the succeeding drawings will be enlarged six times. The second line draws a triangle. Because of the coordinate system changes, it will be translated, rotated, and scaled on each cycle's iteration.

Also, disable the filling mode by inserting the `ofNoFill()` line before the `for` loop.

> The `stripePattern()` function's body should look like the following:

```
ofSetColor( ofColor::black );
ofSetLineWidth( 3.0 );
ofNoFill();
for (int i=-50; i<50; i++) {
  ofPushMatrix();
  ofTranslate( i*20, 0 );
  ofRotate( i*5 );
  ofScale( 6, 6 );
  ofTriangle( 0, 0, -50, 100, 50, 100 );
  ofPopMatrix();
}
```

This results in the pattern in the following figure:

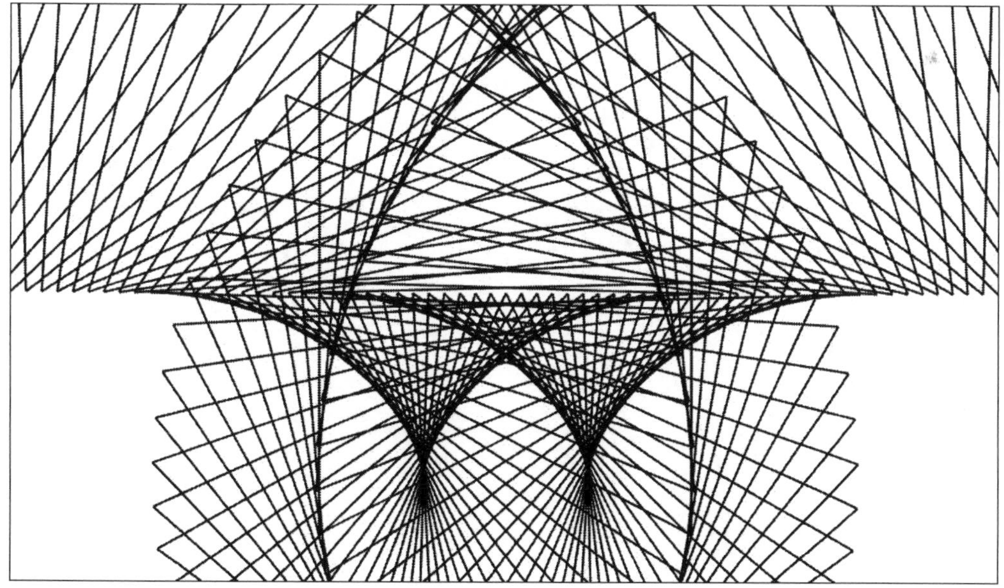

This is a stripe pattern made from triangles

Though formally, it's still a stripe pattern, visually it is not a stripe, but rather a wireframe surface in 3D!

At this point, we are stopping experimenting with the stripe pattern generator. Congratulations, our first openFrameworks 2D drawing project and sketch of the video synthesizer is ready!

> Feel free to tweak the parameters of the code to explore a variety of patterns you can generate with it.
>
> For example, you could alter parameters of `ofScale`... or change `i*20` and `i*5` (in `ofTranslate...` and `ofRotate...`) to some other formulas. Also, you could draw all primitives in different colors by inserting `ofSetColor(...)` into the cycle, with color values, depending on `i`.

Summary

In this chapter, we created a new project and set up its screen size and frame rate. Also, you learned the basics of 2D graphics with openFrameworks by drawing geometric primitives and stripe patterns.

The project we built is a sketch of the video synthesizer. In the next chapter, we will enhance it by adding GUI, which lets us change drawing parameters interactively.

3

Adding a GUI and Handling Keyboard Events

Most of the real-time projects, including video synthesizers, need to be interactive. The simple way to do it is to equip the project with a GUI and handle keyboard events. In this chapter, we will consider how to do this by covering the following topics:

- Creating a GUI with sliders and checkboxes
- Handling keyboard events
- Saving screenshots
- Working with presets
- Using system dialogs to save and load files

Finally, we will implement an advanced method for generating geometric patterns, called **matrix pattern generator**.

Creating a GUI using the ofxGui addon

A GUI is a set of visual elements for controlling an application with mice and keyboards on desktops, and with fingers on mobiles. It includes panels and controls, such as sliders, checkboxes, and buttons.

The simplest way to create a GUI with openFrameworks is using its core addon—`ofxGui`. A typical GUI made with this addon is shown in the following screenshot:

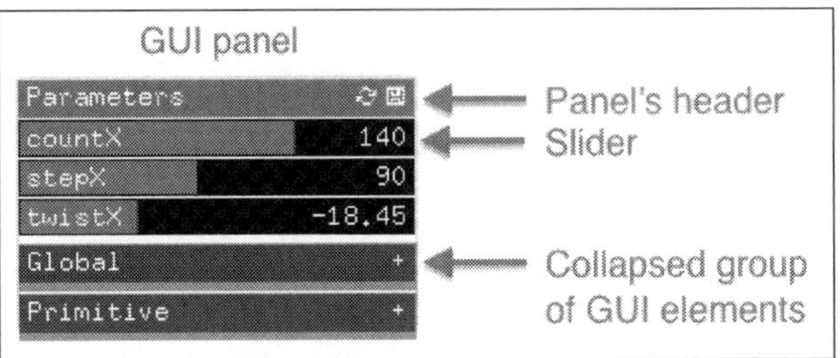

This is a typical GUI created with the ofxGui addon

It is a panel, consisting of a header, a number of sliders, and several groups of visual controls, which can be collapsed to save screen space. Although such a GUI looks minimalistic, it should be quite enough for many experimental and creative projects.

If you want to have a more comprehensive GUI, you can install some other GUI-dedicated addon from `ofxaddons.com` (for example, the `ofxUI` addon), or even use your native OS GUI controls (considering how to do it depends on your OS and is beyond the scope of the book).

Implementing a simple GUI panel with sliders

Let's create a simple GUI consisting of a panel and three sliders. The first thing required is to add the `ofxGui` addon to the project. Fortunately, we already did it when creating the project in the previous chapter (see step 4 (**Selecting the addons**) of the *Creating a project* section of *Chapter 2, Creating Your First openFrameworks Project*). Perform the following steps:

1. Include the addon's header to the `ofApp.h` file by inserting the following line (after the `#include "ofMain.h"` line):

   ```
   #include "ofxGui.h"
   ```

2. Next, declare the visual panel and four sliders by adding the following lines to the `ofApp` class' declaration:

   ```
   ofxPanel gui;
   ofxIntSlider countX;
   ofxFloatSlider stepX;
   ofxFloatSlider twistX;
   ```

The first line declares the GUI panel, which will be a container for all our GUI elements. The second line declares the `countX` slider, which holds integer values. The last two lines declare the `stepX` and `twistX` sliders with float values.

> The `gui`, `countX`, `stepX`, and `twistX` parameters are just object names. They are not associated with some GUI-related structures nor maintained by an IDE (as it happens in some GUI-programming libraries), so you are free to rename them as you want without any problem.

3. Now, add the following code to `ofApp::setup()` to set up declared objects:

```
gui.setup( "Parameters", "settings.xml" );
gui.add( countX.setup( "countX", 50, 0, 200 ) );
gui.add( stepX.setup( "stepX", 20, 0, 200 ) );
gui.add( twistX.setup( "twistX", 5, -45, 45 ) );
```

   The first line sets the title of `gui` to `"Parameters"` and also specifies the name of the XML file for storing the interface elements' values (we will discuss storing a little bit later). In our case, the file name is `"settings.xml"`.

   The next three lines set up sliders and add them to `gui`. For each slider, the arguments of the `setup` method specify the slider's title (for example, for `countX`, it is `"countX"`), its starting value (for `countX`, it is `50`), and its range (for `countX`, it is a range from `0` to `200`).

4. Finally, add the following line to the last line of `ofApp::draw()`:

```
gui.draw();
```

   This function draws the `gui` panel on the screen.

This simple GUI is ready! On running the project, you will see the GUI panel, as shown in the following screenshot:

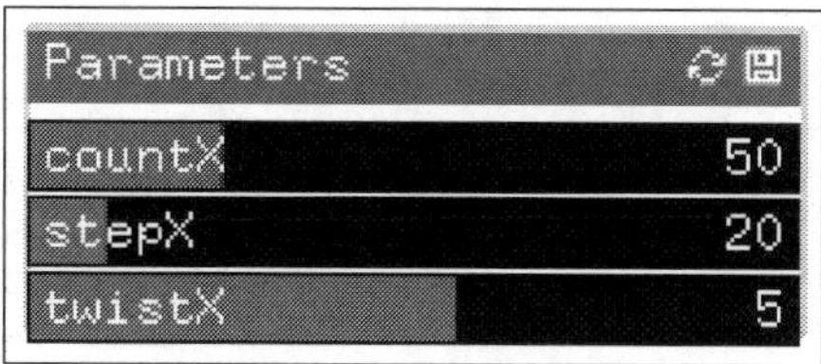

This is a GUI panel with three sliders

The panel is active—you can adjust the sliders' values by clicking on them or dragging them. Also, you can move the panel across the screen by dragging its header. By clicking on the two small buttons on the right-hand side of the header, you can save and load the current state of the sliders to the `settings.xml` file, which will be stored in the `bin/data` folder of the project.

Using the sliders' values

For obtaining the current value of each slider, we can use the slider object itself, as shown in the following code:

```
float f = stepX;
```

This code sets the value of the `stepX` slider to `f`.

Let's use our three sliders' values for parameterizing the `stripePattern()` function, which we implemented in the previous chapter. So, in the body of the `stripePattern()` function, replace the constant values with the sliders' values in the following way:

```
for (int i=-countX; i<=countX; i++) {
  ofPushMatrix();
  ofTranslate( i * stepX, 0 );
  ofRotate( i * twistX );
  ofScale( 6, 6 );
  ofTriangle( 0, 0, -50, 100, 50, 100 );
  ofPopMatrix();
}
```

Now, `countX` controls the number of drawn primitives, `stepX` controls the distance between primitives along the *X* axis, and `twistX` controls the rotation of the primitive depending on its index.

When `stepX` is zero, you will get a *circular pattern*, that is, a pattern obtained by a primitive rotating around some point. When `stepX` is greater than zero, you will get a pseudorandom ornament or a kind of *3D surface*, made from big triangles, as shown in the following image:

This is an image made by adjusting GUI sliders

To generate this particular image, set the sliders' values to `151`, `6`, and `0.899998`.

Playing with the project, very soon you will notice that it would be desirable to have an *autosave* feature, which automatically restores the last state of GUI controls when the project restarts. Let's do it now!

Implementing the autosave feature

Autosaving can be implemented by saving the GUI state to a file when the project ends, and loading the GUI state from this file on project startup. To accomplish this, perform the following steps:

1. Declare the new `exit()` function in the `ofApp` class:

   ```
   void exit();
   ```

2. Then, add its definition to the `ofApp.cpp` file, as follows:

   ```
   void ofApp::exit() {
     gui.saveToFile( "settings.xml" );
   }
   ```

   openFrameworks calls the `exit()` function right before finishing the project. So, this function saves the state of the `gui` elements to the `settings.xml` file, which is located in the `bin/data` folder of the project.

3. To load the `gui` state at startup, add the following line to the end of the `setup()` function:

   ```
   gui.loadFromFile( "settings.xml" );
   ```

Autosave is ready; let's check it! Run the project, move the sliders, and note their values. Now, close the project and run it again. You will see that sliders' values were restored properly.

Now let's extend our GUI capabilities a little bit further by learning how to organize GUI controls in groups.

Creating groups of controls

When the number of visual controls increases, it's a good idea to organize them into groups. Grouping simplifies navigating through parameters and helps to save screen space from cluttering, by collapsing currently unused groups.

The `ofxGuiGroup` class is used to create a group of controls. Let's create such a group consisting of three sliders, which will control the scale, rotation, and background of the image:

1. Add the following lines to the `ofApp` class's declaration:

   ```
   ofxGuiGroup globalGroup;
   ofxFloatSlider Scale;
   ofxFloatSlider Rotate;
   ofxFloatSlider Background;
   ```

   The first line declares a group, and the next lines declare sliders for it.

2. Now set up the group and its controls by adding the following code to the `setup()` function (insert it right before the `gui.loadFromFile...` command):

   ```
   globalGroup.setup( "Global" );
   globalGroup.add( Scale.setup( "Scale", 1, 0.0, 1 ) );
   globalGroup.add( Rotate.setup( "Rotate", 0, -180, 180 ) );
   globalGroup.add( Background.setup("Background",255,0, 255));
   gui.add( &globalGroup );
   ```

   The first line sets the group's title to `"Global"`, the next three lines add sliders to the group, and the last line adds the group to the GUI panel.

Running the project, you will see the panel with the added **Global** group, as shown in the following screenshot:

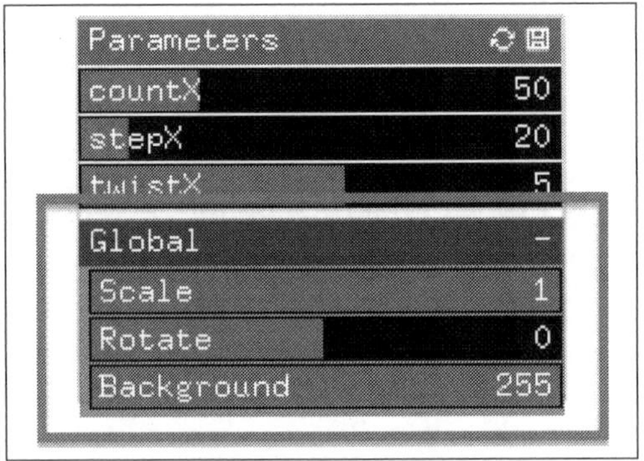

This is a panel with the added Global group of controls

Click on the **-** button located at the right of the group's header to collapse the group. To expand it back, click on the **+** button, which will appear there instead of **-**.

Using the sliders' values

To implement the new sliders' actions, follow these steps:

1. Insert the following line at the beginning of the `draw()` function:

   ```
   ofBackground( Background );
   ```

   This line sets up the background color to a gray color, with brightness specified by the `Background` slider's value.

2. Insert the following lines in the `draw()` function after the `ofTranslate...` line :

   ```
   float Scl = pow( Scale, 4.0f );
   ofScale( Scl, Scl );
   ofRotate( Rotate );
   ```

The first line raises the `Scale` slider's value to the fourth power to control small values of the `Scl` scale more precisely. Indeed, the slider's values from 0.0 to 0.5 will get `Scl` from 0.0 to 0.5*0.5*0.5*0.5 = 0.0625, whereas the slider's values from 0.5 to 1.0 will get `Scl` from 0.0625 to 1. So, you can see that the left half of the slider's values range controls a very small range of `Scl`.

The second and the third lines set up the scale and rotation of the coordinate system.

By running the project, you will see that `Scale` controls the size of the generated image, `Rotate` rotates it, and `Background` sets the brightness of the background.

Implementing a checkbox, a color selector, and a 2D slider

Until now, we have dealt only with float and integer sliders. Let's explore new types of controls: checkbox, color selector, and 2D slider, implemented by the `ofxToggle`, `ofColorSlider`, and `ofVec2Slider` classes, respectively.

There exist classes of controls that are out of the scope of this book. These are the `ofxButton` button class, the `ofxLabel` text label class, and the `ofxVec3Slider` 3D slider class and the `ofxVec4Slider` 4D slider class. See openFrameworks' `gui/guiExample` example for details on using buttons and labels. The 3D sliders work similarly to 2D sliders, which we will consider now.

We investigate them by creating a group of controls to adjust the geometric primitive's drawing parameters:

1. Declare the group and its components in the `ofApp` class's declaration:

```
ofxGuiGroup primGroup;
ofxFloatSlider shiftY, rotate;
ofxVec2Slider size;
ofxColorSlider color;
ofxToggle filled, type;
```

   The first line declares a new group of controls, `primGroup`, and the second line declares two float sliders, `shiftY` and `rotate` (we considered this class previously). The third line declares the 2D slider's `size` parameter. The fourth line declares the color selector, `color`. The last line declares two checkboxes, `type` and `filled`.

2. Now, set them up in `setup()` with the following code (insert it right before the `gui.loadFromFile...` command):

```
primGroup.setup( "Primitive" );
primGroup.add( shiftY.setup("shiftY",0.0,-1000.0,1000.0 ) );
primGroup.add( rotate.setup("rotate",0.0,-180.0,180.0 ) );
primGroup.add( size.setup( "size",
  ofVec2f(6,6),
  ofVec2f(0,0),
  ofVec2f(20,20) ) );
primGroup.add( color.setup( "color",
  ofColor::black,
  ofColor(0,0,0,0),
  ofColor::white ) );
primGroup.add( filled.setup( "filled", false ) );
primGroup.add( type.setup( "type", false ) );
gui.add( &primGroup );
```

   The first three commands set up a group, `primGroup`, and the float sliders, `shiftY` and `rotate` (we considered similar commands earlier). The fourth command sets up the 2D slider's `size` parameter by specifying its title, starting value, and range. Note that value and range are specified using the constructor of the `ofVec2f` class.

The `ofVec2f` class represents a two-dimensional float vector. Objects of this class have the float fields `x` and `y`, which are the vector's components. The class has many useful methods, such as getting vector length and rotating the vector by an angle. See details on the `ofVec2f` class's definition in the `ofVec2f.h` openFrameworks file.

The next command sets up the `color` color selector with its title, starting color (`black`), and range from an empty color (with red, green, blue, and alpha components equal to `0`) to `white`. The next two commands set up checkboxes, `type` and `filled`, by specifying their names and starting values as `false` (that means unchecked). The last line adds the created group, `primGroup`, to the GUI panel.

3. On running the project, you will see the new group, **Primitive**, as shown in this screenshot:

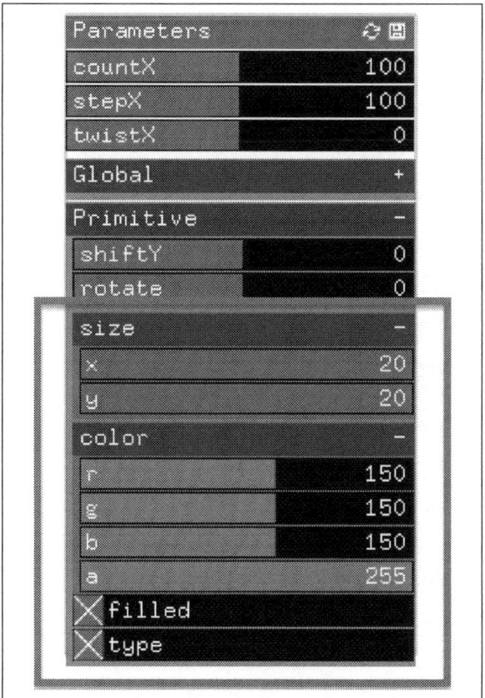

This shows a new group of controls, Primitive, with a 2D slider, a color selector, and two checkboxes

Note that the 2D slider **size** consists of two float sliders **x** and **y**, and the color selector **color** consists of four float sliders, corresponding to all color channels: **r**, **g**, **b**, and **a**.

Using the controls' values

Now let's change the code of the `stripePattern()` function to use the new controls' values. We need to replace the setting color, filling mode, and drawing triangle commands with its parameterized versions. Additionally, let's set the line's width to 1.0 pixel (as we don't need thick contours anymore). So, the function's body will look as follows:

```
ofSetColor( color );
ofSetLineWidth( 1 );
if ( filled ) ofFill(); else ofNoFill();
for (int i=-countX; i<=countX; i++) {
  ofPushMatrix();
  ofTranslate( i * stepX, 0 );
  ofRotate( i * twistX );

  ofTranslate( 0, shiftY );
  ofRotate( rotate );
  ofScale( size->x, size->y );
  if ( type ) ofRect( -50, -50, 100, 100 );
  else ofTriangle( 0, 0, -50, 100, 50, 100 );

  ofPopMatrix();
}
ofScale( 6, 6 );
ofTriangle( 0, 0, -50, 100, 50, 100 );
```

The first command sets the drawing color to the `color` value, the second command sets the drawing line width to `1` pixel (its default value), and the third line sets the filling mode depending on the `fill` value; `fill` is a checkbox, and its value is `true` when checked and `false` when unchecked.

The command for drawing a triangle was changed more radically; it was replaced with five lines of code. Here, the first three lines adjust the local coordinate system for the primitive's drawing in the following way:

- The first line shifts the primitive along the local *Y* axis by the number of `shiftY` pixels. In general, the direction of shifting does not coincide with the *Y* axis of the screen because it depends on the twisting parameter `twistX` and the primitive's index `i`.
- The second line rotates the local coordinate system of the primitive on the rotate angles.
- The third line scales the local coordinate system by the `x` and `y` components of the group of sliders' `size`. This results in changing the width and height of the drawn primitive.

The specifics of the 2D slider

Its x and y values are accessed by ->, in contrast with the usual . (such as size.x and size.y). Normally, in C++, using -> means using the structure dereference operator, and it is used to access the fields of pointers. But, in our case, -> is just an overloaded operator implemented in the ofxVec2Slider class to access its x and y values. Don't care about it and just use it.

Finally, the last two lines draw the square or triangle, depending on the type value.

Experimenting with the project

Now, run the project. Let's explore it:

1. At first, set **countX** to 1. Then, only one primitive will be drawn in the center of the screen. Now, adjust all controls in the **Primitive** group and explore how they affect the primitive's shape and color clarity.
2. Now, increase the value of **countX** to 30 or more, and set non-zero values for **stepX** and **twistX**. Then, a stripe pattern will be generated (we discussed such patterns in the previous chapter). Now change **shiftY** and **rotate** and explore how it affects the geometry of the resulting pattern. If the image seems too black, try to reduce the size of the primitives (by adjusting **size**) or disable filling (by unchecking **fill**).
3. Finally, decrease the **a** component of the **color** field (that is, opaqueness), and explore how primitives are drawn semitransparent. You will obtain the image, as shown in the following screenshot:

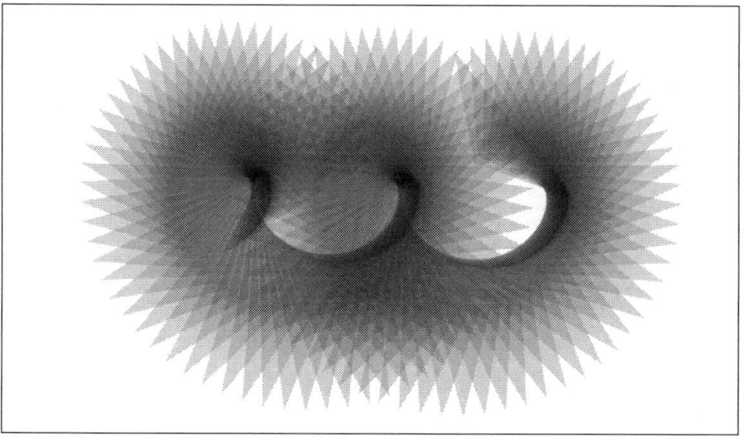

This is an image generated using semitransparent triangles

If you want to reproduce exactly this image, use the parameters shown in this screenshot:

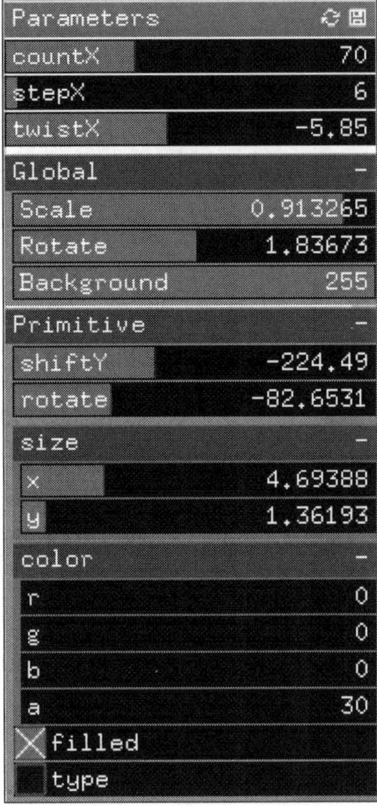

The parameters used to generate the previous image

In this screenshot, the **a** slider is set to **30**, but its slider is invisible on the screen! This is caused by the fact that the **r**, **g**, **b**, and **a** sliders are drawn using the color they constitute; in our case, these are **0**, **0**, **0**, and **30**. This means a semitransparent black color and it is invisible on a black panel's background.

At this point, our video synthesizer is able to generate quite interesting images. But how do we save them? We resolve this question right now by saving screenshots and parameter presets using keyboard events.

Handling keyboard events

The keyboard events are handled by the `keyPressed(int key)` and `keyReleased(int key)` functions, which are called by openFrameworks when a key is pressed and released respectively. The `key` input argument holds the numerical code of the key. Let's implement handling key pressings in our project and use it to add some desirable features: hiding GUI, saving screenshots, and saving/loading presets.

> We consider here only key pressing events. Handling key releasing is implemented in a similar way.

Hiding the GUI

In order to capture the image generated with our project, we need to be able to hide the GUI from the screen. To achieve this, let's define the Boolean variable `showGui`, implement its toggling by pressing *Z*, and use its value to decide whether we should draw `gui` on the screen:

1. Add the variable definition to the `ofApp` class:

   ```
   bool showGui;
   ```

2. Next, set up its starting value in `setup()`:

   ```
   showGui = true;
   ```

3. Now, implement its toggling by inserting the following command in the `ofApp::keyPressed` function:

   ```
   if ( key == 'z' ) showGui = !showGui;
   ```

   This line checks whether *Z* is pressed and then inverts the `showGui` value using the negotiation operator `!` (`true` to `false` and `false` to `true`).

4. Finally, add the `showGui` value checking to make a decision on drawing `gui` by replacing the `gui.draw();` command in the `draw()` function with this one:

   ```
   if ( showGui ) gui.draw();
   ```

Run the project. Now, by pressing *Z* (lowercase *z* key), the GUI will disappear from and appear back on screen.

Saving a screenshot

Let's save a screenshot to an image file by pressing *Return* (*Enter*). Add the following line to the `keyPressed` function:

```
if ( key == OF_KEY_RETURN ) ofSaveScreen( "screenshot.png" );
```

> Note that the *Return* (*Enter*) control key in openFrameworks is denoted as `OF_KEY_RETURN`. All other control keys begin with `OF_KEY_` too. For example, `OF_KEY_LEFT` means the left cursor key.

The `ofSaveScreen` function saves the screen content to a file. In our case, it is `screenshot.png`, located in the `bin/data` folder of the project.

> If you want to save screenshots to files with different names, the simplest way to achieve it is to use a random number generator to choose filenames. Replace "`screenshot.png`" with the following code:
>
> ```
> "screenshot" + ofToString(ofRandom(0, 1000), 0) +
>   ".png"
> ```
>
> Then, screenshots will be saved to files with a name of the type `screenshotX.png`, where `X` is a number from 0 to 999, for example, `screenshot359.png`. This code is based on using the `ofRandom(0, 1000)` function, which generates floats from `0` to `1000` (and the result is strictly less than `1000`). This float value is converted to a string using the `ofToString` function. Its second argument `0` means that we need no digits after the period. So, we get a string representing an integer number from 0 to 999. Next, it is concatenated with the `screenshot` and `.png` strings to obtain the desired random filename.

Saving a preset using the system save dialog

The set of values of all the project's parameters is called a **preset**. Saving and loading presets are crucial features of any creative software project. In our case, all important project parameters are values of GUI controls and can be saved to and loaded from a file using the `gui.saveToFile` and `gui.loadFromFile` functions.

Let's implement saving a preset to a file by pressing *S*. The filename will be chosen using the system save dialog. Add the following code to the `keyPressed` function:

```
if ( key == 's' ) {
  ofFileDialogResult res;
  res = ofSystemSaveDialog( "preset.xml", "Saving Preset" );
  if ( res.bSuccess ) gui.saveToFile( res.filePath );
}
```

The first line of code checks whether *S* is pressed. If it's true, then the second line declares the `res` variable, which will hold the system save dialog result. The third line executes the saving dialog with the starting filename as **preset.xml** and title as **Saving Preset**. In the fourth line, we check whether the dialog was successful, and save the current state of the `gui` parameters to the selected file.

In the current version of openFrameworks for Windows, arguments of `ofSystemSaveDialog` do not affect the appearance of the system dialog; it appears with an empty starting filename and with a generic title.

Now, run the project and press *S* to save your preset to a file. You will see a dialog for choosing a file to save the preset. When it succeeds, your preset, that is, the current GUI controls' values will be saved to that file.

Loading a preset using the system load dialog

Let's implement loading a preset by pressing *L* with the following code:

```
if ( key == 'l' ) {
  ofFileDialogResult res;
  res = ofSystemLoadDialog( "Loading Preset" );
  if ( res.bSuccess ) gui.loadFromFile( res.filePath );
}
```

It is like a code for saving a preset, but instead of saving, it loads the GUI controls' values.

Run the project, press *L*, and in the appeared dialog, choose a file where you saved your preset before. The preset will be loaded.

Implementing the matrix pattern generator

Perfect! We've explored creating a GUI with the `ofxGui` addon and covered some of its quirks.

In this final section, we don't want to investigate any new GUI topics but wish to implement an advanced algorithm for drawing geometric patterns.

If you feel that you have achieved your goal in programming GUI and don't want to improve the pattern generation algorithm right now, we'd suggest that you skip this section and proceed to the next chapter.

We will do this by adding four new sliders and creating a new function to draw a matrix pattern (we will explain it in the following paragraphs). When this succeeds, our video synthesizer will be able to generate a very wide range of pictures, ranging from VJ-style patterns to vivid *organic* shapes, as shown in these screenshots:

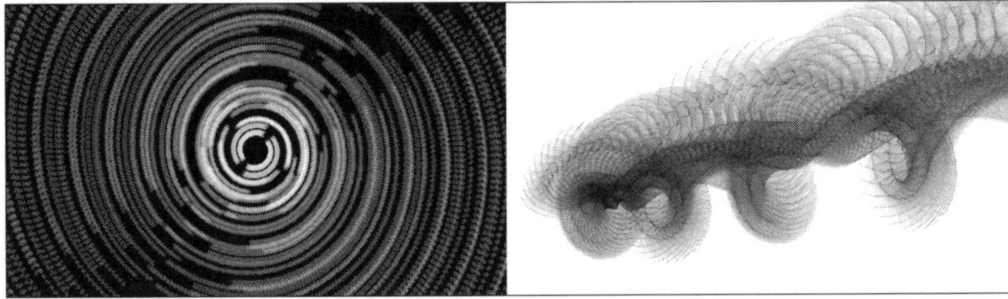

These are examples of images generated with the matrix pattern generator

You will be able to generate these two images in your project using the values given in the end of the section.

A **matrix pattern** is a geometric pattern that is obtained by drawing many copies of some stripe pattern, with shifting, scaling, and rotating (see the theory of stripe patterns in the *The stripe pattern* section of *Chapter 2, Creating Your First openFrameworks Project*). It is named "matrix pattern" because it consists of a number of geometric primitives with their centers lying on a (geometrically twisted) matrix:

1. To implement it, add the four sliders and a `matrixPattern` function definition to the `ofApp` class:

   ```
   ofxIntSlider countY;
   ofxFloatSlider stepY, twistY, pinchY;
   void matrixPattern();
   ```

2. Now set up the sliders by inserting this code right before the `globalGroup.setup...` command:

```
gui.add( countY.setup( "countY", 0, 0, 50) );
gui.add( stepY.setup( "stepY", 20, 0, 200 ) );
gui.add( twistY.setup( "twistY", 0, -30, 30 ) );
gui.add( pinchY.setup( "pinchY", 0, 0, 1 ) );
```

3. On running the project, you will see the GUI with new sliders, as shown in this screenshot:

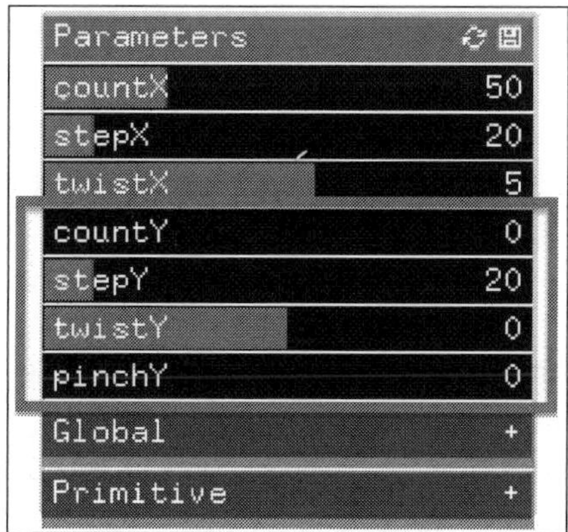

This shows a panel with added matrix pattern generator's controls

Using the sliders' values

Now, let's code the `matrixPattern` function. This function will draw `1+2*countY` stripe patterns, by shifting them at `stepY` pixels along the *Y* axis and rotating by `twistY` degrees. Also, the `pinchY` slider will adjust the scale of each stripe in the pattern depending on its index. Insert the function's code to the `ofApp.cpp` file:

```
void ofApp::matrixPattern() {
  for (int y=-countY; y<=countY; y++) {
    ofPushMatrix();
    //---------------------
    if ( countY > 0 ) {
      float scl = ofMap( y, -countY, countY, 1-pinchY, 1 );
      ofScale( scl, scl );
    }
    ofTranslate( 0, y * stepY );
    ofRotate( y * twistY );
    stripePattern();
    //---------------------
    ofPopMatrix();
  }
}
```

The function consists of the `for` cycle, which executes `1+2*countY` times. The body of the cycle stores the current coordinate system by calling the `ofPushMatrix` function, and then scales, translates, and rotates it, depending on the sliders' values. Next, it calls the `stripePattern` function to draw the stripe pattern and finally restores the original coordinate system.

To understand the code, at first consider the case where `countY` is equal to zero. Then, the cycle executes once with `y = 0`. The `countY > 0` condition will fail, so `ofScale` will not call, and the `ofTranslate` and `ofRotate` functions will do nothing, because `y` is equal to zero. Calling `stripePattern` draws the original stripe pattern without any coordinate system change. Hence, in the case of `countY = 0`, `matrixPattern` just draws a stripe pattern.

Now, consider the case `countY > 0`. In this case, the `ofScale`, `ofTranslate`, and `ofRotate` functions will change the coordinate system depending on the index `y`, and a stripe pattern will be drawn `1+2*countY` times.

The `ofMap` function is new in code. This function performs *linear interpolating* of `y` from range `[-countY, countY]` to range `[1-pinchY, 1]`. That is, when `y` is equal to `-countY`, it returns `1-pinchY`; when `y` is equal to `countY`, it returns `1`. For intermediate `y` values, it returns linearly increased floats between `1-pinchY` and `1`. The result of this function is stored to the `scl` variable and used to scale the coordinate system in the next line of code. So, we obtain a linearly increased sequence of `scl` scales, depending on `y`. Here, the `pinch` value controls the range of stripe scales. In particular, when `pinch` is equal to `0`, all the `scl` values are equal to `1`; when `pinch` is equal to `1`, the `scl` values linearly run from `0` to `1`.

The last thing remaining is to call the `matrixPattern` function. Locate the following line in the `draw()` function::

```
stripePattern();
```

Replace this line with:

```
matrixPattern();
```

The matrix pattern generator is ready! Let's learn to use these new drawing capabilities.

Experimenting with the matrix pattern generator

Start checking the matrix pattern generator by creating a simple matrix pattern, consisting of 25 squares, as shown in the following screenshot:

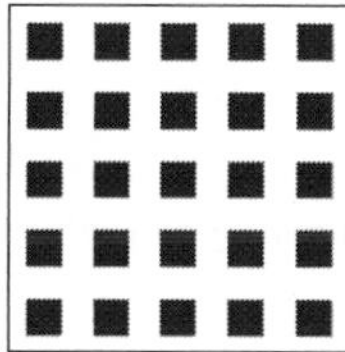

This is a simple matrix pattern

To get it, set the GUI controls to the following values:

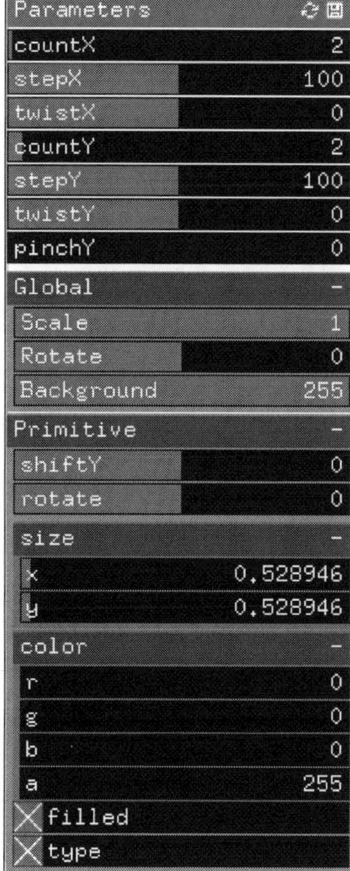

These are the values for generating a simple matrix pattern

Then, change the added `countY`, `stepY`, `twistY`, and `pinchY` sliders to see how they affect the pattern's geometry.

When you have generated an interesting image, don't forget to save its preset to the file by pressing *S*. Then you will be able to use and probably improve it in the future!

If you want to reproduce the two example images shown at the beginning of this section, use the following values:

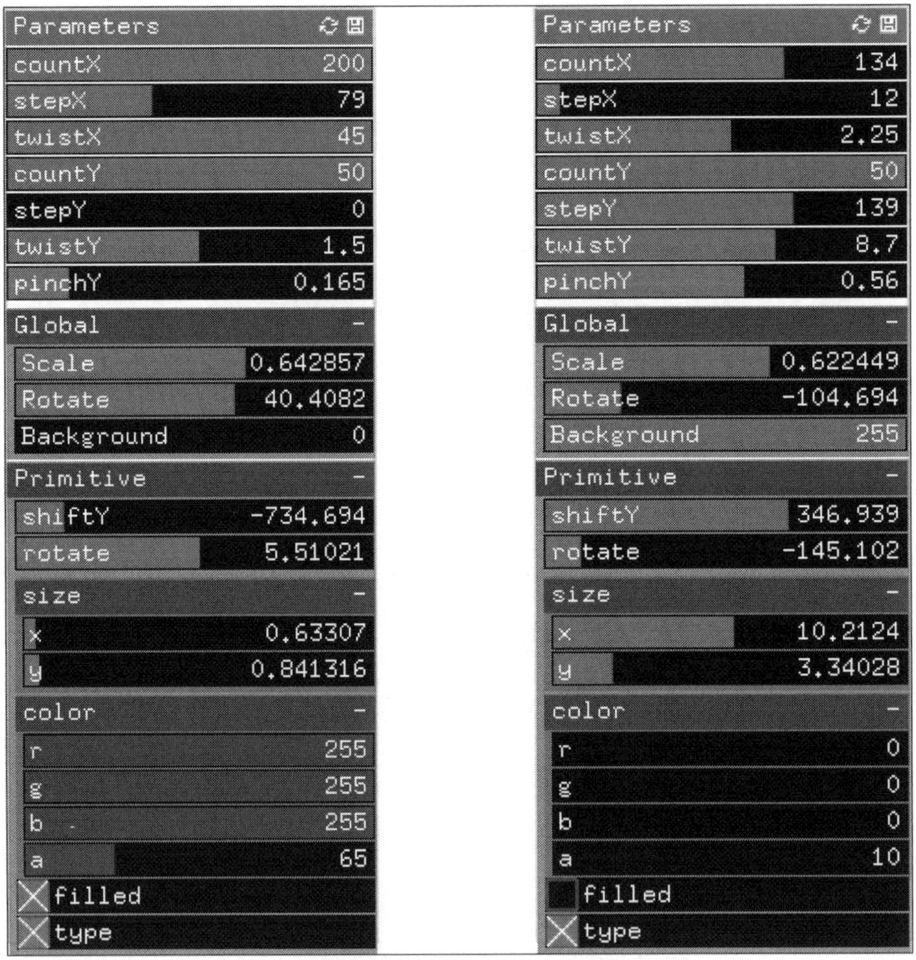

Parameters		
countX	200	134
stepX	79	12
twistX	45	2.25
countY	50	50
stepY	0	139
twistY	1.5	8.7
pinchY	0.165	0.56
Global	-	-
Scale	0.642857	0.622449
Rotate	40.4082	-104.694
Background	0	255
Primitive	-	-
shiftY	-734.694	346.939
rotate	5.51021	-145.102
size	-	-
x	0.63307	10.2124
y	0.841316	3.34028
color	-	-
r	255	0
g	255	0
b	255	0
a	65	10
filled	X	
type	X	X

These are the values for generating example images

Summary

In the chapter, we built the GUI for controlling all parameters of the project and added handling the keyboard events to save screenshots and working with presets. Also, we significantly improved a drawing algorithm by implementing the matrix pattern generator.

At this point, we have quite a functional project for generating elaborate 2D visuals made from geometric primitives.

This project we created could be called a light version of the video synthesizer. We will deploy it on mobile devices in *Chapter 8, Deploying the Project on iOS, Android, and Raspberry Pi*. So, we recommend that you back up the current state of the project (for example, by archiving project's folder to a ZIP file) before you go on to the next chapter.

In the next chapter, we will extend our graphics capabilities using images and videos and process them with shaders.

4
Working with Raster Graphics – Images, Videos, and Shaders

In the previous chapters, we dealt with 2D graphics made exclusively from geometric primitives. This kind of graphics is called **vector graphics** and is great for generating algorithm-based pictures. Drawing and manipulating pictures of real-world objects requires other 2D graphics called **raster graphics**, which is based on raster images.

In this chapter, we will consider the basics of raster graphics by covering the following topics:

- Loading and drawing raster images and videos
- Grabbing and drawing live video from a camera
- Mixing images using additive blending
- Drawing to the offscreen buffer
- Processing images using fragment shaders demonstrated by implementing the kaleidoscope effect.

At the end of the chapter, we will have our video synthesizer extended with raster graphics capabilities, including mixing images, video files, and live video from a camera, and processing the resulting picture with the kaleidoscope effect.

Raster images in openFrameworks

A **raster image** is a rectangular array of **pixels**. To keep things short, we will call a raster image an image.

Each pixel holds color information represented by one or several numerical values. This number of values is called a **number of channels** of the image. openFrameworks supports the images with one, three, and four numbers of channels:

- A one-channel image is called a **grayscale image**. Its pixels hold brightness values.
- A three-channel image is called a **color image**. Its pixels hold red, green, and blue components of the color.
- A four-channel image is called a **color image with alpha channel**. Its pixels have an additional component, alpha, controlling the transparency of the pixels.

openFrameworks supports loading from and saving images to all popular image file formats, including PNG, JPG, BMP, and TIFF.

There are three classes for working with images:

- `ofImage`: This is intended for manipulating the pixel values and drawing an image
- `ofPixels`: This is intended for manipulating the pixels values only
- `ofTexture`: This is intended for drawing images only

The `ofImage` class is the most universal image class. The `ofPixels` and `ofTexture` classes are specialized for particular usage (pixel manipulation or drawing) and consumes less memory comparing with `ofImage`.

In fact, the `ofImage` object contains one `ofPixels` object and one `ofTexture` object that are automatically synchronized.

Drawing an image file

Let's load an image file and draw it on the screen. We will not want to change the pixel values, so we will use the `ofTexture` class for this task. Perform the following steps:

1. Add the image object definition to the `ofApp` class:

```
ofTexture image;
```

2. Add the command for loading the image from the `collage.png` file to `setup()`:

   ```
   ofLoadImage( image, "collage.png" );
   ```

3. At the beginning of the `draw()` function, right after the `ofBackground...` command, add the code for drawing the image:

   ```
   ofSetColor( 255 );
   image.draw( 0, 0, ofGetWidth(), ofGetHeight() );
   ```

   The first line sets up the white drawing color, which serves here as an image drawing color (see the details about the `ofSetColor` function in *Chapter 2, Creating Your First openFrameworks Project*). By setting the color to white, we are guaranteed that the image will be drawn without color change.

> Setting another color will lead to changing the appearance of the image on the screen. For example, if we use the `ofSetColor( 0, 255, 0 )` command (which sets the drawing color green), only the green channel of the image will be drawn.

The second line draws the image on the screen, with the top-left corner position (`0, 0`), width `ofGetWidth()`, and height `ofGetHeight()`. As a result, the image will be drawn stretched on the whole screen.

> If we specify only the first two arguments in the `image.draw...` command, such as `image.draw(0, 0)`, the image will be drawn in its own size.

4. Finally, copy the `collage.png` image file to the `bin/data` folder of the project. You can get the file from the archive provided with the book.

> **Credits**
>
> We made this image file, `collage.png`, by collating several nature photos by:
>
> - ©iStockphoto.com/wojciech_gajda
> - ©iStockphoto.com/thawats
> - ©iStockphoto.com/magnetcreative
> - ©iStockphoto.com/yuliang11
> - ©iStockphoto.com/chantalrutledge

On running the project, you will see the `collage.png` image stretched to the screen and some geometric pattern over it (which we implemented in previous chapters). To hide the geometric pattern for a moment, set its **color a** slider to zero. You will see the following picture:

This is an image, collage.png, drawn by our project

Playing a video file

openFrameworks supports video files of various formats, including MP4, MOV, and AVI. The class for playing videos is `ofVideoPlayer`.

> For playing videos with openFrameworks on Windows, you need to have Apple's QuickTime installed. It's free to download from `apple.com`. (Please, restart Windows after installing.)

Let's load a video file and play it on the screen in the following way:

1. Add the video object definition to the `ofApp` class:

   ```
   ofVideoPlayer video;
   ```

2. Add the commands to load the video from the `flowing.mp4` file and starting it to play by inserting the following lines to `setup()`:

   ```
   video.loadMovie( "flowing.mp4" );
   video.play();
   ```

3. Add the command to update video objects regularly by inserting the following line to `update()`:

   ```
   video.update();
   ```

This command manages the loading of new video frames when it is needed, so we should call it regularly to have proper and smooth video playback.

4. Add the commands to draw the current video frame by inserting the following lines to `draw()`, right after the `image.draw...` command:

```
ofSetColor( 255 );
video.draw( 0, 0, ofGetWidth(), ofGetHeight() );
```

This code sets the drawing color to white and draws a video frame stretched on the screen.

5. Finally, copy the `flowing.mp4` video file to the `bin/data` folder of the project. You can get the file from the archive provided with the book.

We made this video by animating colored geometric figures and applying to it motion blur effect several times.

On running the project, you will see the video played on the screen, as shown in the following screenshot:

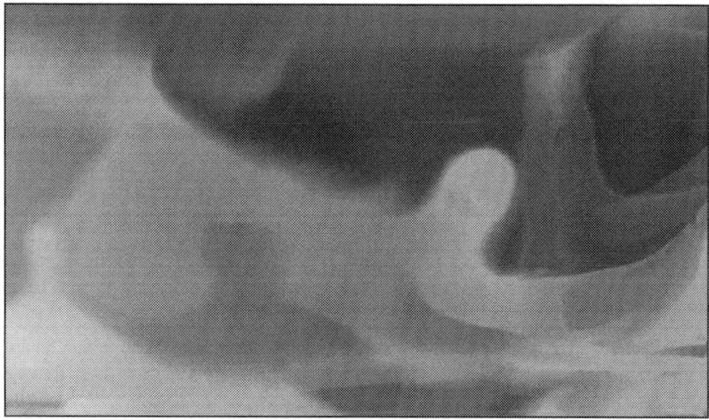

This is a video flowing.mp4 played by our project

Having video playback is good, but currently, it completely occludes the image drawn in the previous section! Don't worry. A little later, we will implement the video mixer to control the appearance of the image and video.

But, before doing that, let's implement grabbing video from a camera.

Grabbing a live video from a camera

openFrameworks can grab live video from a built-in or external camera connected to your computer. It is accomplished using the `ofVideoGrabber` class.

Let's implement starting the camera to grab and draw the grabbed video frames on the screen.

> Starting a camera can take several seconds. Thus, if we start it in `setup()`, the project will take a bit longer to start. It could be quite annoying to keep the camera "on" even when we don't use it. For this reason, we will start the camera only when we need it, by pressing C.

The following are the implementation steps:

1. Add the grabber object definition to the `ofApp` class:

   ```
   ofVideoGrabber camera;
   ```

2. Add the commands to start the camera by adding the following lines to `keyPressed()`:

   ```
   if ( key == 'c' ) {
     camera.setDeviceID( 0 );
     camera.setDesiredFrameRate( 30 );
     camera.initGrabber( 1280, 720 );
   }
   ```

   The first line is a condition checking whether C is pressed. The second line selects the camera device by its identifier, which is a number starting with zero. If you have only one built-in or external connected camera, it has a zero identifier. The next (following) connected cameras will have the identifiers 1, 2, and so on.

   The third line sets the frame rate of the camera grabbing to 30 FPS. Finally, we start the camera by calling the `initGrabber` method specifying the required video frame size; in our example, it is a width of `1280` pixels and a height of `720` pixels.

3. Add the command to update the camera grabber regularly by inserting the following line to `update()`:

   ```
   if ( camera.isInitialized() ) camera.update();
   ```

   This code checks whether the camera has actually started, and if so, updates it.

The `camera.update()` command manages the grabbing of new video frames, so we should call it regularly to have proper grabbing.

4. Add the commands to draw the last grabbed video frame by inserting the following lines to `draw()` after the `video.draw...` command:

```
if ( camera.isInitialized() ) {
  ofSetColor( 255 );
  camera.draw( 0, 0, ofGetWidth(), ofGetHeight() );
}
```

   This code checks whether the camera is actually started, and if so, sets the drawing color to white and draws a video frame stretched on the screen.

On running the project and pressing *C*, the camera will start grabbing, and after a couple of seconds, you will see the grabbed video on the screen, as shown in the following screenshot:

A video grabbed by our project

Mixing layers using additive blending

At this point, we draw four graphical layers:

- Image file
- Video file
- Video from camera
- Geometric pattern generator (developed in two previous chapters)

The first three layers are simply drawn occluding each other. Only the fourth layer has control of its transparency (**color a** slider), so we can hide and show it back smoothly.

To control the visibility of the first three layers, let's create a video mixer. It will be a new GUI group, **Mixer**, consisting of three sliders, adjusting layers' transparencies. Additionally, we will draw the layers using a special mixing mode called **additive blending**. It's a mixing mode where drawing colors at each pixel are summed up to obtain the resultant picture.

> Additive blending models the behavior of physical light. Imagine that we output each layer to separate the physical projector. If we point all the projectors to one area on the wall, the resulting picture will be just the sum of all the projectors' lightings. This is exactly how additive blending works.

The remarkable property of such mixing is independent of the drawing order of layers.

> By default, openFrameworks uses the **alpha blending** mode, which mixes up colors depending on the order of drawing and the colors' transparencies. Alpha blending models how light is reflected from a stack of pictures drawn on the glass. This mode is especially appropriate for creating collages with several layers.

Creating the mixer's GUI

Let's implement the mixer's GUI elements:

1. Declare a new GUI group and three sliders in the `ofApp` class :

   ```
   ofxGuiGroup mixerGroup;
   ofxFloatSlider imageAlpha, videoAlpha, cameraAlpha;
   ```

2. Add the commands to set up the GUI group to `setup()` after the `gui.add( &primGroup )` line:

   ```
   mixerGroup.setup( "Mixer" );
   mixerGroup.setHeaderBackgroundColor( ofColor::darkRed );
   mixerGroup.setBorderColor( ofColor::darkRed );
   ```

   The first line sets up the group name **Mixer**. The next two lines set up the header color and background color of the group to dark red, so this group will be better distinguished from the other controls in the GUI.

3. Add sliders to our group (continue to insert lines to `setup()`):

```
mixerGroup.add( imageAlpha.setup( "image", 100,0,255 ) );
mixerGroup.add( videoAlpha.setup( "video", 200,0,255 ) );
mixerGroup.add( cameraAlpha.setup( "camera", 100,0,255 ) );
```

4. Collapse all the previously added groups and add our group to the GUI panel (continue to insert lines to `setup()`):

```
gui.minimizeAll();
gui.add( &mixerGroup );
```

The `gui.minimizeAll()` command collapses all the currently existing groups in the `gui` panel. By contrast, as the new `mixerGroup` group is added to `gui` after this command, it will appear expanded.

On running the project, you will see the new **Mixer** GUI group colored in dark red. It appears expanded, whereas **Global** and **Primitive** groups appear collapsed, as shown in the following screenshot:

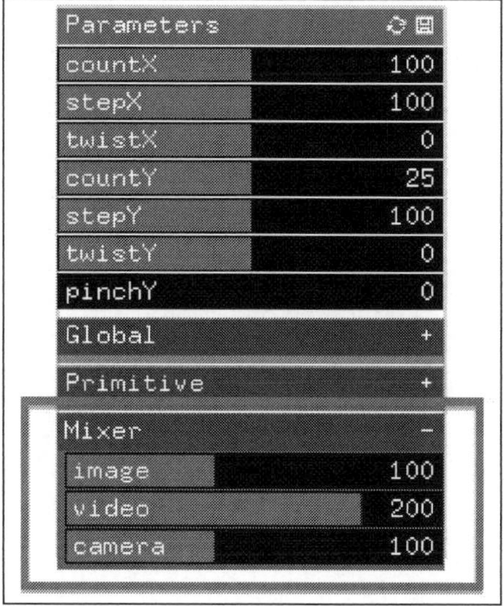

This shows a new Mixer group of controls

Implementing the mixer's functionality

Now, we will use the slider's values to control the transparency of drawing layers and enable the additive blending mode. Perform the following steps to accomplish this:

1. Go to the `draw()` function text, and find the following block of code that draws the image, video, and camera:

   ```
   ofSetColor( 255 );
   image.draw( 0, 0, ofGetWidth(), ofGetHeight() );
   ofSetColor( 255 );
   video.draw( 0, 0, ofGetWidth(), ofGetHeight() );
   if ( camera.isInitialized() ) {
     ofSetColor( 255 );
     camera.draw( 0, 0, ofGetWidth(), ofGetHeight() );
   }
   ```

2. Replace each `ofSetColor...` command with the following commands that set the drawing color to white with transparency depending on the sliders' values:

   ```
   ofSetColor( 255, imageAlpha );
   ...
   ofSetColor( 255, videoAlpha );
   ...
   ofSetColor( 255, cameraAlpha );
   ...
   ```

The `ofSetColor( v, a )` command sets the red, green, and blue components of the drawing color to v, and its alpha component to a. See the details on the `ofSetColor` function in *Chapter 2, Creating Your First openFrameworks Project*.

3. Next, add a command to enable additive blending before this block, and add a command to enable the alpha blending mode back after this block, as follows:

   ```
   ofEnableBlendMode( OF_BLENDMODE_ADD );
   ...
   ofEnableAlphaBlending();
   ```

4. Finally, the whole drawing block will look like the following code:

   ```
   ofEnableBlendMode( OF_BLENDMODE_ADD );
   ofSetColor( 255, imageAlpha );
   image.draw( 0, 0, ofGetWidth(), ofGetHeight() );
   ```

```
ofSetColor( 255, videoAlpha );
video.draw( 0, 0, ofGetWidth(), ofGetHeight() );
if ( camera.isInitialized() ) {
  ofSetColor( 255, cameraAlpha );
  camera.draw( 0, 0, ofGetWidth(), ofGetHeight() );
}
ofEnableAlphaBlending();
```

The mixer is ready! Run the project. You will see the image and video blended with each other, as shown in the following screenshot:

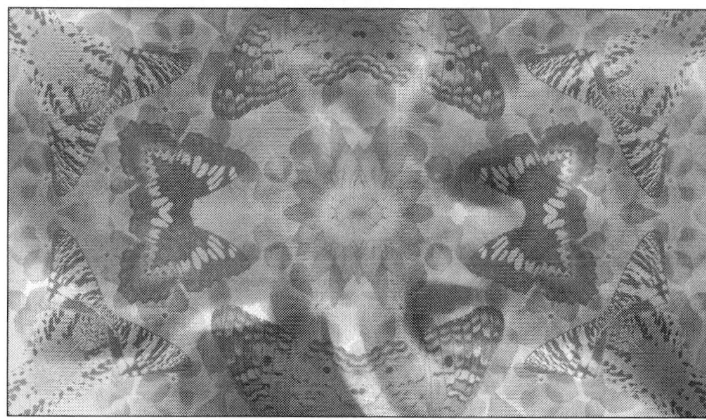

This shows the image and video mixed with additive blending

Don't be afraid if you see a blank white screen! That means that your project is currently drawing a white background. Drawing anything over the white background with additive blending mode gives white screen, and that's what you see. To resolve the issue, just set the **Background** slider to `0`.

Press *C* to activate the camera too. Now, adjust sliders in the **Mixer** group to mix the image, video, and camera, and adjust the **color a** slider in the **Primitive** group to mix the pattern generator over it.

While the first three layers are drawn with additive blending, the fourth layer—pattern generator—is drawn using alpha blending. So, it is overlying on the screen not by adding, but as an opaque or semitransparent picture (depending on **color a** slider's value).

Creating the video effect with a shader

Now, we will demonstrate processing a video using shaders. We do it by implementing the well-known **kaleidoscope** effect. This effect is quite generic, and its implementation exhibits many things that you would need to create your own effects with shaders.

> Shaders are tiny programs executed on GPU (video card). A video effect implemented with shaders works faster than its CPU-based analogue. This is the reason for shaders for being the most popular technology for creating real-time video effects.

Shaders are written in the **GLSL** language. It is a specialized version of the C language, containing a number of built-in functions and variables.

There are several types of shaders, including **vertex**, **fragment**, and **geometry** shaders. Here, we are interested in a shader that allows us to change the colors of the drawn pixels. The most appropriate shader type for such a task is **fragment shader**. Such a shader is executed by the video card to process each pixel right before drawing it. While executing, the shader can change the color of the drawn pixels, and it's just what we need to create video effects.

To process an image with a fragment shader, at first we need to enable the shader, then send the image to drawing, and finally disable the shader.

In our case, the image we want to process is the picture of the entire screen generated by our project. Unfortunately, there is no straightforward way to obtain the screen contents as an image. To achieve this, we will use a special technique called **offscreen buffer**. Let's discuss it.

Redirecting drawing to the offscreen buffer

The **offscreen buffer** is a *virtual screen* in video memory, where we can draw anything just as we can on a real screen. The resultant picture can be used as an image or texture. We can draw it on a real screen, process with shader, or use to texture 3D objects.

In the OpenGL library, which is used by openFrameworks for drawing, the offscreen buffer is called **Frame Buffer Object** (**FBO**). Naturally, in openFrameworks, this buffer is maintained by the `ofFbo` class.

Let's use this class to redirect our drawing to the offscreen buffer by performing the following steps:

1. Declare the offscreen buffer in the `ofApp` class:

   ```
   ofFbo fbo;
   ```

2. Allocate the buffer in `setup()`:

   ```
   fbo.allocate( ofGetWidth(), ofGetHeight(), GL_RGB );
   ```

   The first and the second arguments set up the dimensions of the buffer. The last argument, `GL_RGB`, specifies that the buffer should hold the pixels colors only (red, green and blue components), without alpha channel.

> The `GL_RGB` value should be passed as a third argument of `the fbo.allocate...` command when `fbo` is used as a substitute for the real screen (which has no alpha channel). Another possible value is `GL_RGBA`, which means a color with the alpha channel. It is used when the buffer's contents need to hold alpha values, for example, for layering it over other graphics using alpha blending.

3. Move all the drawing code from `draw()` to the new `draw2d()` function, that is, declare a new function `draw2d()` in the `ofApp` class:

   ```
   void draw2d();
   ```

4. Then, insert its empty definition to `ofApp.cpp`:

   ```
   void ofApp::draw2d(){
   }
   ```

5. Move all the code of the `draw()` function to this new function, except the last line:

   ```
   if ( showGui ) gui.draw();
   ```

6. Redirect all the drawing to `fbo` by inserting the following lines at the beginning of the `draw()` function:

   ```
   fbo.begin();
   draw2d();
   fbo.end();
   ```

   The first line enables redirection of the drawing to `fbo`, the second line performs the drawing, and the last line disables redirection of the drawing to `fbo`, that is, it redirects the drawing back to the real screen.

Great! Now all the drawing, except the GUI, is redirected to the offscreen buffer. Thus, on running the project, you will see just the blank screen with GUI.

We want to mention one important difference between the screen and the offscreen buffers: the buffer is not cleared automatically to the background color at each frame. Such behavior can be useful to create accumulated graphics, such as particle trails. In our case, the offscreen buffer `fbo` will be cleared at each frame by calling `ofBackround`, which is the first command in the `draw2d` function's body.

Note that for the same purpose, you could use the command `ofClear`, which clears the offscreen buffer (or screen), such as `ofBackground`, but does not affect the background color used for clearing the screen. The arguments for calling `ofClear` are the same as for `ofBackground`.

Drawing the offscreen buffer contents and enabling smoothing

Let's draw the offscreen buffer contents on the screen to check whether it works properly. Add the following lines to `draw()` after the `fbo.end()` command:

```
ofSetColor( 255 );
fbo.draw( 0, 0, ofGetWidth(), ofGetHeight() );
```

The first line sets the drawing color to white, and the second line draws the buffer on the screen as though it were drawing images.

Now the `draw()` function should look like the following:

```
fbo.begin();
draw2d();
fbo.end();
ofSetColor( 255 );
fbo.draw( 0, 0, ofGetWidth(), ofGetHeight() );
if ( showGui ) gui.draw();
```

By running the project, you will see the same picture you did before implementing the offscreen buffer.

It seems all is good. But, wait for a moment. Increase the **color a** slider value and look in detail at the picture made by the pattern generator. Note that the lines look a bit crude. Actually, they are *aliased*, as shown in the following screenshot:

This shows aliased lines

The reason for this is the fact that drawing to the real screen uses the antialiasing capabilities of the video card that aren't implemented by default in FBOs.

We can resolve this problem easily by manually enabling line smoothing.

When line smoothing is enabled, all lines are drawn antialiased. But, filled shapes keep drawing aliased. To resolve the issue and draw all graphics antialiased, we need to perform drawing to a bigger FBO and then draw its contents to the screen smoothly; the details of this method are out of this book's scope.

Doing this, we need to take into consideration an additional fact. Currently, smoothing in openFrameworks doesn't work together with additive blending. So, it is necessary to disable smoothing before enabling additive blending and enable it back right after additive blending is finished, in the following way:

1. Insert the command to disable smoothing in `draw2d()`, right before the `ofEnableBlendMode( OF_BLENDMODE_ADD )` command:

   ```
   ofDisableSmoothing();
   ```

2. Insert the command to enable smoothing, right after the `ofEnableAlphaBlending()` command in `draw2d()`:

   ```
   ofEnableSmoothing();
   ```

On running the project (and unchecking the **filled** checkbox for drawing line contours), you will see that lines become smooth, as shown in the following screenshot:

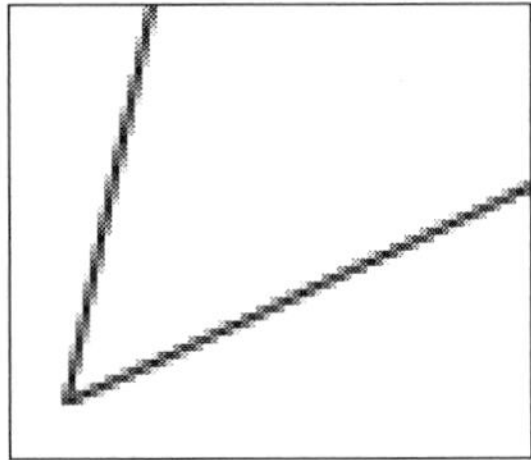

This shows antialiased lines

Now, we are ready to pass the buffer's contents to shader processing!

Implementing the kaleidoscope effect

Let's implement the **kaleidoscope effect**. This effect takes a circular sector of an input image and draws its copies around the screen center. It results in ornamental images, such as the one shown in the following screenshot:

This shows the kaleidoscope effect

To accomplish this, we will do three things:

1. Create the fragment shader at the file `kaleido.frag`. This file will contain the algorithmic core of the effect.
2. Create the vertex shader in the file `kaleido.vert`. This file will contain a simple vertex shader needed for fragment shader to work properly.
3. Load and use shaders created in the project.

Creating the fragment shader

Create a new text file called `kaleido.frag` in the `bin/data` folder of the project using your IDE or any available text editor.

Fill it with code by performing the following steps:

1. Add generic directives:

   ```
   #version 120
   #extension GL_ARB_texture_rectangle: enable
   ```

   The first line specifies that we are using GLSL version 1.20.

   > Though 1.20 is quite an old version of GLSL, it's currently used in most of the built-in openFrameworks examples. This version is simple to learn and is enough to implement many video effects.

   The second line enables working with textures of arbitrary size (not only powers of two, which is assumed by default).

2. Add definitions of the constants π and 2π:

   ```
   #define PI (3.14159265358979323846)
   #define TWO_PI (2*PI)
   ```

   We will use these constants in the following code.

3. Specify input parameters of the shader using the `uniform` keyword:

   ```
   uniform int ksectors = 10;
   uniform float kangleRad = 0.0;
   uniform vec2 kcenter = vec2( 1280.0, 720.0 ) / 2.0;
   uniform vec2 screenCenter = vec2( 1280.0, 720.0 ) / 2.0;
   uniform sampler2DRect inputTexture;
   ```

   The first parameter `ksectors` is an integer value, denoting a number of kaleidoscope's sectors. The second parameter `kAngleRad` is a float value, denoting the rotation angle of the kaleidoscope's grabbed segment, measured in radians. The third and the fourth parameters `kcenter` and `screenCenter` are two-dimensional vectors, denoting the center of the kaleidoscope's grabbed segment and the screen center coordinates in pixels. The last parameter defines the internal name of the image we are processing: `inputTexture`.

4. Define the `main()` function:

```
void main(){
  vec2 texCoord = gl_TexCoord[0].xy;
  vec2 v = texCoord - screenCenter;
  float r = length( v );
  float a = atan( v.y, v.x );

  float A = TWO_PI / float(ksectors);
  a = mod( a, A );
  if ( a > A/2.0 ) a = A - a;
  a -= kangleRad;

  vec2 u = vec2( cos(a), sin(a) ) * r;
  u += kcenter;
  gl_FragColor = texture2DRect( inputTexture, u );
}
```

That's all, our fragment shader is ready! Let's explain the `main()` function in detail.

How it works

The shader's `main()` function is called by the graphics card for each pixel right before drawing it. This function should set a predefined GLSL variable, `gl_FragColor`, to some value, which is the color the graphics card will actually draw in the pixel.

Color in GLSL is represented as a four-dimensional vector `vec4` with components `r`, `g`, `b`, `a` (red, green, blue and alpha). The color components are float values lying in the range of 0 to 1. For example, the command:

```
vec4 color = vec4( 1.0, 0.0, 0.0, 1.0 );
```

puts the red opaque color to `color`.

Our `main()` function does the following:

- The first line sets the two-dimensional vector `texCoord` equal to the current texture coordinates of the processed pixel using the predefined GLSL variable `gl_TexCoord`. Index `[0]` indicates that we are getting texture coordinates from the default (zero) texture. A *swizzling* access to a vector component, `.xy`, is used in GLSL, which means here that we are creating two-dimensional vector made from the `x` and `y` components of `gl_TexCoord[0]`.
- The second line sets the vector `v` to the difference between `texCoord` and the screen center vector `screenCenter`.

- The third line sets the variable `r` to the length of `v` using the built-in GLSL `length` function.
- The fourth line sets variable `a` to the angle between the *X* axis and `v`, measured in radians, using the built-in GLSL function `atan`.

  Now the values `r` and `a` represent `v` in polar coordinates with the center of coordinates at `screenCenter`, as shown in the following diagram:

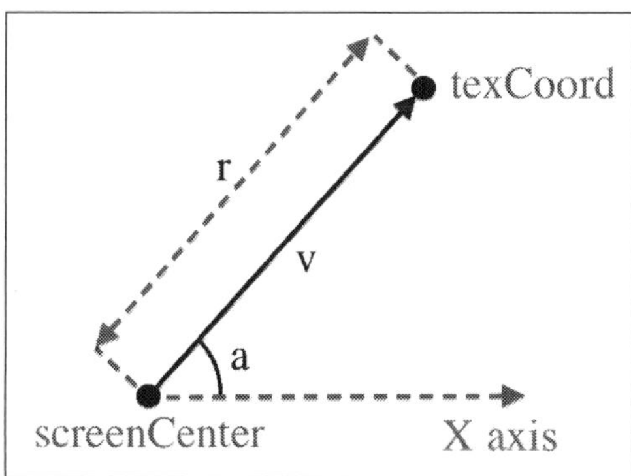

This is a representation of the vector v in the polar coordinates r and a

- The next block of four lines transforms angle `a`. The line `float A = ...` computes the angular size `A` of one kaleidoscope's sector, measured in radians. It is the angle of the whole circle 2π divided by the number of sectors `ksectors`. The integer value `ksectors` is converted into a float value to avoid GLSL compilation errors, which can appear on some video cards.
- The next line `a = mod( a, A )` sets `a` equal to `a` modulo `A`. This means wrapping the original value of `a` to a range from `0` to `A`. This is the most important command for creating the kaleidoscope's effect.
- The next line `if ( a>A/2.0 )...` mirrors the value `a` over value `A/2` in cases where `a` exceeds `A/2`. As a result, our kaleidoscope will have sectors filled with symmetrical pictures.
- The line `a += kangleRad` shifts `a` by `kangleRad` radians. Thus `kangleRad` is the rotation of the sector grabbed from the input image.
- Finally, the last block of three lines computes the output color of the shader. The first line constructs the vector `u` having the length `r` and rotated from the *X* axis by the angle `a`.
- The next line shifts `v` by `kcenter`. Thus, `kcenter` is the center of the sector grabbed from the input image.
- The last line sets the `gl_FragColor` GLSL variable to the color of the input image `inputTexture` at the point `u`.

The fragment shader is created. It was the most important thing for the implementation of the effect. The two smaller things that remain to be done are creating the vertex shader and incorporating shaders in the project.

Creating the vertex shader

To execute any fragment shader, it is required to have a *companion* , that is, a vertex shader. A vertex shader transforms the attributes of processed vertices, such as the position and texture coordinates. It works before the fragment shader.

> In the context of shaders, **vertices** mean the vertices of all drawn figures. For example, when we are drawing an image, it is implemented in openFrameworks as drawing a textured rectangle, so in this case, four vertices will be processed (the image's corners).

In our example, it's enough to have a simple vertex shader, which passes vertices without any transformation.

Create a new text file called `kaleido.vert` in the `bin/data` folder of the project, and fill it with the following code:

```
#version 120
void main() {
  gl_Position = gl_ModelViewProjectionMatrix * gl_Vertex;
  gl_TexCoord[0] = gl_MultiTexCoord0;
  gl_FrontColor = gl_Color;
}
```

The first line specifies that we are using GLSL version 1.20. The next line defines the `main()` function, which is called by the video card to process each vertex. The body of the function consists of three lines, which set up vertex position, texture coordinates, and a drawing color in a generic way.

Using created shaders in the project

Let's load and use the fragment and vertex shaders in the openFrameworks project. We do it by employing the `ofShader` class. Additionally, we will create several GUI controls to be able to adjust the shader's parameters. So, perform the following steps:

1. Add the shader's object and GUI controls declarations to the `ofApp` class:

   ```
   ofShader shader;
   ofxToggle kenabled;
   ofxIntSlider ksectors;
   ofxFloatSlider kangle, kx, ky;
   ```

The first line declares the `shader` object for dealing with shaders. The next lines declare the GUI controls: the `kenabled` checkbox to enable and disable the shader, the `ksectors` integer slider to control the number of kaleidoscope's sectors, and the `kangle`, `kx`, and `ky` float sliders that control the grabbed sector's rotation angle and center position.

2. After the `mixerGroup.add( cameraAlpha...` command, add the commands for loading the shader and setting up the GUI controls to `setup()`:

```
shader.load( "kaleido" );
mixerGroup.add( kenabled.setup( "kenabled", true ) );
mixerGroup.add( ksectors.setup( "ksectors", 10, 1, 100 ) );
mixerGroup.add( kangle.setup( "kangle", 0, -180, 180 ) );
mixerGroup.add( kx.setup( "kx", 0.5, 0, 1 ) );
mixerGroup.add( ky.setup( "ky", 0.5, 0, 1 ) );
```

The first line loads the vertex and fragment shaders from the `kaleido.vert` and `kaleido.frag` files (which are expected to be in the `bin/data` folder of the project). Also, the shaders are compiled.

Shaders are compiled by a video card driver. If a compiling error occurs, they are printed to console without stopping the project's execution.

The next lines set up the GUI checkbox and four sliders and add them to the `mixerGroup` group.

3. Right before the `fbo.draw...` command, add commands for enabling the shader and passing parameters to it in `draw()`:

```
if ( kenabled ) {
  shader.begin();
  shader.setUniform1i( "ksectors", ksectors );
  shader.setUniform1f( "kangleRad", ofDegToRad(kangle) );
  shader.setUniform2f( "kcenter", kx*ofGetWidth(),
    ky*ofGetHeight() );
  shader.setUniform2f( "screenCenter", 0.5*ofGetWidth(),
    0.5*ofGetHeight() );
}
```

When the `kenabled` checkbox is checked, this code enables the shader by the `shader.begin()` command and then sets the shader's parameters `ksectors`, `kangleRad`, `kcenter`, and `screenCenter` with values from the corresponding sliders. Note that the `kcenter` and `screenCenter` parameters are two-dimensional vectors, so we pass two values, the first for the x vector component and the second for the y vector component.

The last two symbols in the `setUniformXX` command means the type and number of components of the parameter we set to the shader. In the considered code, we set the integer scalar (`1i`), float scalar (`1f`) and two-dimensional float vector (`2f`) parameters using the `setUniform1i`, `setUniform1f`, and `setUniform2f` commands respectively. To see all available variants of this command, see the definition of the `ofShader` class.

The next command after this block of code in `draw()` is the `fbo.draw...` command. It draws the `fbo` buffer contents on the screen. If the shader was enabled, then `main()` function of `kaleido.frag` will be executed for each pixel of the drawn picture. The `gl_FragColor` color generated by this function will be actually drawn on the screen. So, the contents of `fbo` will be drawn with the applied kaleidoscope effect.

4. Now we need to disable the shader. Add the following line after the `fbo.draw...` command:

```
if ( kenabled ) shader.end();
```

This command disables the shader if it was enabled earlier.

Great, we just completed implementing the kaleidoscope effect!

Run the project and check the **kenable** checkbox to enable the kaleidoscope. You will see that part of the screen's picture will be repeated around the screen center, as shown in the following screenshot:

Here the kaleidoscope effect is applied to the image collage.png

Now, adjust the kaleidoscope's sliders to see how they affect the resultant picture. Then, adjust all other GUI controls. After a while, you will find that the kaleidoscope effect, together with the video mixer and the pattern generator, is able to produce a myriad beautiful ornaments!

If you want to reproduce a kaleidoscopic picture, which is shown at the beginning of the *Implementing the kaleidoscope effect* section, set the GUI controls to the following values:

Slider	Value
Background (in the **Global** group)	`0`
color a (in the **Primitive** group)	`0`
image	`255`
video	`80.6633`
camera	`0`
kenabled	`checked`
ksectors	`40`
kangle	`-7.34694`
kx	`0.19898`
ky	`0.346939`

Summary

In this chapter, we considered the basics of raster graphics. We began with loading and drawing raster images and video files and also captured video from a camera. Then, we implemented the video mixer, which mixes all these pictures using additive blending. Next, we directed all drawing to the offscreen buffer and processed its contents with the shader-based kaleidoscope effect.

With this chapter, we are done with considering the basics of 2D graphics in openFrameworks. Now, we have a video synthesizer, which generates 2D vector graphics, mixes it with raster graphics, and processes the resultant picture with the shader effect.

In the next chapter, we will explore a different kind of graphics—3D graphics. We will draw the sphere surface in 3D and will use our 2D graphics to texture it and deform its shape.

5

Creating 3D Graphics

3D graphics is a technique for representing 3D objects and drawing them on a 2D screen. It extends 2D graphics, which we considered in previous chapters, using a number of new notions, including the 3D coordinate system, *Z*-buffering, camera object, lighting, and texturing. In this chapter, we will consider the basics of 3D graphics in openFrameworks by discussing these new notions and covering the following topics:

- Drawing a wireframe, solid, and textured sphere
- Deforming and extruding a sphere
- Mixing 2D and 3D graphics

As a result, we will obtain a colorful and fancy 3D sphere on the screen.

Introduction to 3D graphics with openFrameworks

3D graphics is based on using the three-axes coordinate system (*X*, *Y*, *Z*). The *X* and *Y* coordinates are directed in exactly the same way as in 2D's case, and the additional *Z* axis is perpendicular to the screen plane and directed at us.

> Actually, openFrameworks draws everything as 3D graphics. When we draw anything using 2D drawing commands, just as we did in the previous chapters, openFrameworks uses Z as being equal to zero.

Most of openFrameworks' 2D drawing functions that we already know have their similar 3D counterparts. For example, consider the commands:

```
ofLine( 10, 20, 30, 40, 50, 60 );
ofTriangle( 100, 200, 300, 400, 500, 600, 700, 800, 900 );
```

These will draw a line segment between the points with coordinates (`10, 20, 30`) and (`40, 50, 60`) and a triangle with vertices (`100, 200, 300`), (`400, 500, 600`), and (`700, 800, 900`).

To simplify the code, you can use the `ofPoint` class, which represents a 3D point or vector. It has the fields `x`, `y`, `z`, and a number of handy geometric methods, such as `length()` (getting the length of a vector). Using this class, we can rewrite the command for drawing a triangle as the following:

```
ofPoint a(100, 200, 300);
ofPoint b(400, 500, 600);
ofPoint c(700, 800, 900);
ofTriangle( a, b, c );
```

Apparently, such code is much more elegant. Note that in some openFrameworks functions, the second name of this class is used: `ofVec3f` (which means *vector with three float components*). Both names are equivalent for use.

Other useful examples are translating and scaling the coordinate system. Let's take a look at the following commands:

```
ofTranslate( 0, 0, 100 );
ofScale( 1, 1, 2 );
```

This will shift the coordinate system towards us by Z at `100` units and zooms the coordinate system in the Z direction by factor `2`.

openFrameworks classes for surface representation

3D graphics is more demanding to memory and computing power than 2D graphics. The reason for that is the necessity to represent the whole object's surface to be able to observe it from all the possible views. For example, to draw a cube with 2D graphics, we need to draw no more than *three* quadrangles, as shown in the following image:

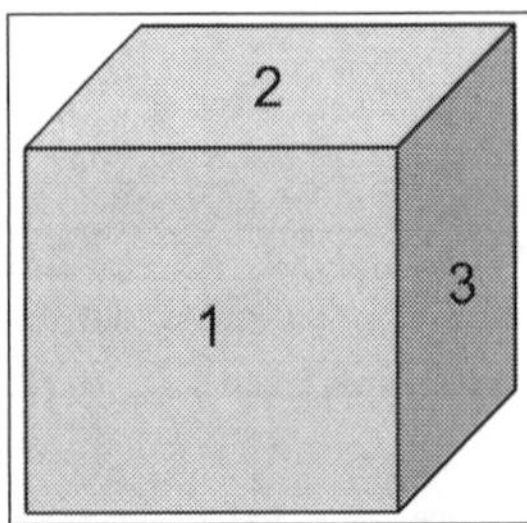

To draw a cube in 2D graphics, no more than three quadrangles are needed

But to represent a cube as a 3D surface, we need *six* squares, one for each cube's side.

To handle this demand, the optimization techniques for the representation and fast drawing of 3D objects should be used. In openFrameworks, this demand is solved by several classes:

- `ofMesh`: This is a universal class to represent and draw a polygonal surface made from triangles. Such a surface is called a **triangular mesh**. Also, `ofMesh` can represent a collection of lines or a set of points.
- `ofVboMesh`: This is an analogue of the `ofMesh` class, which is accelerated using the **Vertex Buffer Object** (**VBO**) technology.
- `ofPlanePrimitive`, `ofSpherePrimitive`, `ofIcoSpherePrimitive`, `ofCylinderPrimitive`, and `ofConePrimitive`: These are classes that represent particular surfaces made from triangles: rectangular surfaces, spheres, regular spheres made by equal triangles, cylinders and cones, respectively. They are made from one (rectangle, spheres), two (cone (side and cap)) or three meshes (cylinder (side and two caps)).

In this chapter, we will consider working with the `ofSpherePrimitive` class. In the *Deforming by formulas* section, we will show how to get access to its `ofMesh` object and change the vertices of the surface. To see more examples of using all the mentioned classes, see openFrameworks' the `3d/3DPrimitivesExample` and `3d/meshFromCamera` examples.

Drawing a wireframe sphere

Let's start working with 3D by creating a sphere surface and drawing it as a **wireframe model**.

A **wireframe model** is a type of graphical representation of a 3D object on the screen where only its edges are drawn. It appeared in the early era of 3D graphics as a simple way to draw objects in 3D. Now, it is used in 3D modeling software to control the structure of the created objects and as a special effect in films, games, and experimental graphics.

We will achieve this using the `ofSpherePrimitive` class in the following way:

1. Add the sphere object definition to the `ofApp` class, as follows:

```
ofSpherePrimitive sphere;
```

2. Initialize the sphere in `setup()`:

   ```
   sphere.set(250, 20);
   ```

   Here, the first argument, `250`, is the radius of the sphere. The second argument, `20`, is the resolution of the sphere. The resulting spherical surface will have `20` meridians and 20 - 1 = 19 parallels.

   To obtain a smoother sphere, increase `20` to a larger value, for example, to `40`.

3. Draw the sphere using the `sphere.drawWireframe()` command. It is good to add this line not to `draw()` but in a new function. The reason for this is that during the rest of the chapter, we will add new commands related to drawing the sphere, and it will be convenient to write all of them in a separate function. Let's name it `draw3d()`. Declare it in the `ofApp` class, as follows:

   ```
   void draw3d();
   ```

   Add it's definition to ofApp.cpp in the following way:

   ```
   void ofApp::draw3d() {
     ofSetColor( ofColor::white );
     sphere.drawWireframe();
   }
   ```

   The first command in the function body sets up the white color, and the second line draws the sphere in the wireframe mode.

4. Call our new function by inserting the following command before `if ( showGui ) gui.draw();`, which is the last line of `draw()`:

   ```
   draw3d();
   ```

On running the project, you will see the sphere in the top-left corner of the screen. The reason for this issue is that the sphere's center is by default *X=Y=Z=0*, and this is exactly the top-left corner of the screen.

Set the **Background**, **color a**, **image**, **video**, and **camera** sliders to zero to obtain a black screen under the sphere.

Let's place the sphere at the center of the screen. For such a purpose, we could use the `setGlobalPosition` method, which moves the center of the sphere to a specified location in the following way:

```
sphere.setGlobalPosition( ofGetWidth()/2, ofGetHeight()/2, 0 );
```

But a better approach for us is to add a 3D camera object. It automatically moves the center of the coordinates to the screen center and also gives additional capabilities for rotating, rescaling, and moving the 3D scene by mouse. Let's do it.

Creating a camera

One of the advantages of 3D graphics over 2D graphics is the possibility of walking through the virtual scene and rotating objects in a way we do in real life. So the user feels as though he or she were inside that scene, observing *real* objects. The navigating in space is achieved using a *camera*. It is a special object that controls the way of projecting 3D points to 2D points on the screen.

There are two types of projections from 3D to 2D:

- **Perspective projection**: Far-off objects look smaller than nearby objects. This is the type of projection used in openFrameworks by default.
- **Orthogonal projection**: The visible size of an object does not depend on the distance to the viewer.

In openFrameworks, a camera can be represented by the `ofCamera` class or the `ofEasyCam` class. The first class is a quite general camera class, and the second one extends it by implementing a number of additional capabilities, including handling mouse events for controlling the camera.

To enable orthogonal projection for a camera object of the `ofCamera` class or the `ofEasyCam` class, use its `enableOrtho()` method.

Let's implement the `ofEasyCam` object by performing the following steps:

1. Declare the camera object in the `ofApp` class in the following way:

   ```
   ofEasyCam cam;
   ```

2. Activate the camera by inserting the following command at the beginning of `draw3d()` function:

   ```
   cam.begin();
   ```

3. Finally, deactivate the camera by inserting the following command at the end of the `draw3d()` function:

   ```
   cam.end();
   ```

The camera is ready! Upon running the project, you will see the sphere in the screen center, as shown in the following screenshot:

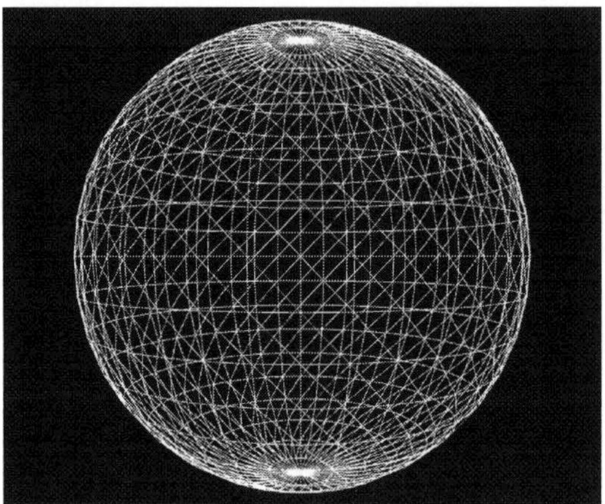

This is a wireframe sphere

The camera reverses the orientation of the *Y* axis, so it is directed up. Be aware about this as it can flip your images vertically. To resolve this issue, you can use the following command, which flips the *Y* axis:

```
ofScale(1, -1, 1);
```

Controlling the camera with a mouse

You can control the camera with a mouse in the following ways:

- *Rotate the scene* by dragging with the left mouse button in any direction
- *Scale the scene* by dragging with the right mouse button up and down
- *Move the scene* by dragging with the middle mouse button in any direction
- *Restore the original camera state* by double-clicking

Playing a little with the project, you would notice one issue. When you adjust sliders in the GUI, the camera responds to this by undesirably rotating the scene. Resolving this issue is easy, and we will do it in the next section.

We note this issue in openFrameworks 0.8.4. Most probably, it will be fixed in the later openFrameworks versions. Hence, if the issue doesn't appear in your project, then no fixing is needed, so skip the next section.

Disabling mouse control for the camera when the GUI is visible

The simple way to eliminate undesirable responses of the camera when adjusting GUI controls with a mouse is disabling mouse control for the camera when the GUI is active and the user has pressed the mouse inside the GUI area, and enabling when the GUI is hidden.

To achieve this, insert the following lines to the `ofApp::mouseMoved(int x, int y)` function:

```
if ( showGui && x < 250 ) cam.disableMouseInput();
else cam.enableMouseInput();
```

This function is called by openFrameworks when the user moves the mouse over the screen. The input parameters `x` and `y` are coordinates of the current mouse position. In our case, if GUI is enabled and `x` is less than `250` (this is slightly bigger than the *X* coordinate of the right border of the GUI panel on the screen), then we disable mouse control for the camera; otherwise, we enable it.

The issue is resolved. Run the project and verify that the camera responds to the mouse only when the mouse position is to the right of the GUI. Note that the considered method works only while the GUI panel is placed in the left-hand side of the screen. (If you drag the GUI panel to the right, the disabling of the camera will not work properly.) Nevertheless, the used method is simple and quite enough for us.

[Now, we will discuss camera automation. This section is supplementary, so you can skip it if you currently aren't interested in camera automation.]

Camera automation

Sometimes, it is desirable to have a camera that moves automatically. For a such a purpose, you can use the camera's `orbit()` method. The method sets the camera's position relative to some point of interest by specifying longitude angle, latitude angle and radius value, as if the camera is a satellite observing Earth. The method is very useful when a camera should fly around and observe some point.

To check how it works, add the following code to the beginning of `draw3d()`:

```
float time = ofGetElapsedTimef();
float longitude = 10*time;
float latitude = 10*sin(time*0.8);
float radius = 600 + 50*sin(time*0.4);
cam.orbit( longitude, latitude, radius, ofPoint(0,0,0) );
```

The first line gets time in seconds from the project starting. The second line sets the longitude angle increasing with time. The third line sets the latitude angle and radius value to values, periodically depending on time. The last line calls the `orbit` method, which sets desired parameters to the camera with the point of interest (`0`, `0`, `0`), which is the center of the coordinate system and the center of our sphere.

Upon running the project, you will see the rotating sphere, which periodically swings and moves nearer and further away.

Drawing a solid sphere

Drawing a surface in the wireframe is a good way to check the structure of the triangle mesh forming the surface. In the context of video synthesis, it can be seen as a kind of special effect. But normally we are interested in drawing a 3D object as *solid surfaces*, which means that all its triangles are drawn as solid polygons.

To draw a solid sphere, just replace the `sphere.drawWireframe()` command in `draw3d()` with the following command:

```
sphere.draw();
```

On running the project, you will see the sphere as a white circle, as shown in the following screenshot:

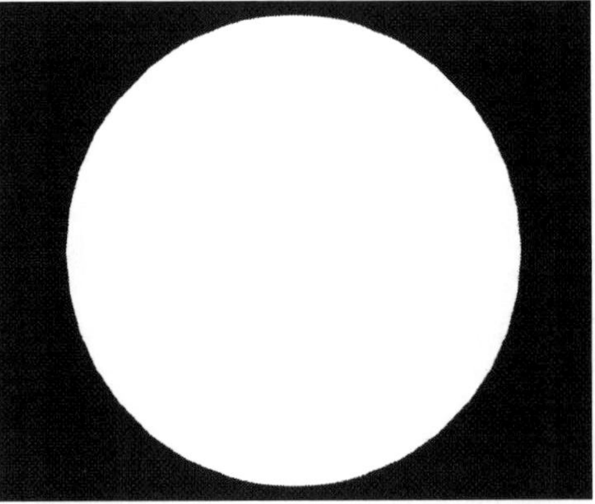

This is a solid sphere without shading.

The reason for the sphere to look like a flat figure is that each triangle in the sphere is drawn as a solid white polygon without using information of its orientation for shading.

To obtain a sphere that looks more natural, let's implement the shading of its surface.

The things needed for shading the surface

To draw a shaded surface, the following things are required:

- **Light source**: The light source models the emission of light from some point. In openFrameworks, the light source is implemented by the `ofLight` class.
- **Material**: The material specifies the properties of light reflection from the surface. In openFrameworks, it is implemented by the `ofMaterial` class.
- **Normals**: The normal in a given surface's point is a vector of unit length directed perpendicular to the surface. It controls the geometry of light reflection. To specify a surface's lighting properties completely, the normals need to be set in all the vertices of the surface. Fortunately, `ofSpherePrimitive` (and other `of...Primitive` classes) set normals automatically during the surface's initialization, so here we don't need to take care of it.
- **Z-buffering**: This is a technique used to decide which parts of the scene are visible and which are hidden on the screen. A special buffer called **Z-buffer** (also known as **depth buffer**) holds the *Z* value for each drawn screen's pixel. Some point *P* from a polygon projected to a screen pixel (*X*, *Y*), will be drawn on the screen only if the *Z* coordinate of *P* is greater than the current value of *Z*-buffer at (*X*, *Y*). (In this case, the *Z*-buffer value at (*X*, *Y*) will be updated with the new *Z* value.)

  By default, *Z*-buffering is disabled in openFrameworks. It is enabled by calling `ofEnableDepthTest()` and disabled back by calling `ofDisableDepthTest()`.

Drawing a solid sphere with shading

Following the items listed in the previous section, let's implement the light source and material, and enable *Z*-buffering for our sphere drawing:

1. Declare a light source and a material object in `ofApp`, as follows:

```
ofLight light;
ofMaterial material;
```

Of course, you can declare several lights and materials and name them in any way you wish.

2. Set the light source's position, then activate it and material, and enable Z-buffering by adding the following commands at the beginning of the `draw3d()` function:

   ```
   light.setPosition(ofGetWidth()/2, ofGetHeight()/2, 600);
   light.enable();
   material.begin();
   ofEnableDepthTest();
   ```

   The first command places the light source at `600` pixels in the Z direction from the screen center. The second command activates the light source and also automatically enables *lighting mode* (that is, the mode for drawing shaded surfaces with lights, materials, and normals). The third command activates the material. Finally, the last command enables Z-buffering.

> Just as in real life, you can enable several different light sources. Then, the total lighting of the scene will be a sum of all the enabled lights. But you can use only one material enabled at a moment. Until you disable it, it will be applied to all the drawn objects. To use another material for drawing, you should deactivate the current material and activate another one.

3. Deactivate the Z-buffering, material, and lighting components by adding the following commands at the end of the `draw3d()` function:

   ```
   ofDisableDepthTest();
   material.end();
   light.disable();
   ofDisableLighting();
   ```

   The first command disables Z-buffering. The second and the third commands deactivate the material and the light source respectively. The last line disables lighting mode. Note that though lighting mode was enabled automatically when we called `light.enable()`, to disable it, calling only `light.disable()` is not enough (this command disables only a particular light source). So we need to call a special function for it, `ofDisableLighting()`. After this, the project is ready to draw 2D graphics again.

> Normally, you should disable Z-buffering when you draw 2D graphics (as well as when drawing 3D transparent objects or using the additive blending mode). In the opposite case, some of the drawn objects will be erroneously discarded by Z-buffering.

On running the project, you will see the shaded sphere, as shown in the following screenshot:

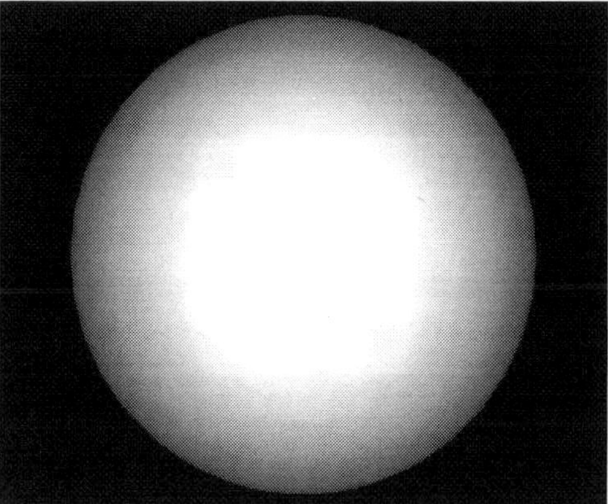

This shows a solid sphere with shading

Now it looks like a real 3D object!

If you rotate the camera using mouse, you will note that the light source is not moving. The reason for this is that it is positioned outside of the block where the camera is active (the camera is active between the `cam.begin()` and `cam.end()` commands). If you want to make the light source position synchronized with a camera, place the following lines after the `cam.begin()` command:

```
light.setPosition(0, 0, 600);
light.enable();
```

These lines set the light position and enable it in a way we did before, but the coordinates of the camera now are (`0, 0`) because the camera centers the coordinate system.

For debugging purposes, you can visualize the light source as a small sphere using the command `light.draw()`.

In this section, we touched upon the very basics of shading with openFrameworks. For more information on adjusting light sources and materials, see the openFrameworks examples, `gl/singleLightExample` and `gl/multiLightExample`.

Now let's texture the sphere.

Texturing the sphere

Texturing is the technique to wrap a 2D image on a surface. In this case, the surface is called **textured surface**, and the image using for texturing is called **texture**.

Texturing involves the following three steps:

1. The first step is preparing the texture image as an `ofTexture` object. We explored this class in the previous chapter. All the considered image and video classes—`ofImage`, `ofVideoPlayer`, `ofVideoGrabber`, and `ofFbo`—contain an `ofTexture` object instance that can be accessed by the `getTextureReference()` method. For example, `video.getTextureReference()` gets the `ofTexture` object for a current frame of video.
2. Setting *texture coordinates* at each vertex of the surface is the second step. Texture coordinates at the given vertex indicate the point in the texture that should be wrapped at this vertex. Fortunately, `ofSpherePrimitive` and other `of...Primitive` classes have the `mapTexCoords` method, which sets texture coordinates; we will use it.
3. The third step is activating texturing for a surface before drawing it and deactivating after the surface is drawn.

Let's go through these steps by texturing the sphere with a picture of the screen, generated by our project during the previous chapters.

Preparing a texture

At first, let's capture a picture of the screen to the offscreen buffer (see the details on this kind of buffer in the previous chapter):

1. Declare a new offscreen buffer object in the `ofApp` class:

   ```
   ofFbo fbo2;
   ```

2. Allocate the buffer in `setup()` by inserting the following line after the `sphere.set...` command:

   ```
   fbo2.allocate( ofGetWidth(), ofGetHeight(), GL_RGB );
   ```

3. Add the `fbo2.begin()` and `fbo2.end()` commands around the commands that enable the kaleidoscope effect, and draw graphics through it:

   ```
   fbo2.begin();
   if ( kenabled ) {
     shader.begin();
   ...
   if ( kenabled ) shader.end();
   fbo2.end();
   ```

   These commands redirect drawing from the screen to the `fbo2` buffer and back.

Now, we can access the texture containing the screen's picture using the `fbo2.getTextureReference()` method.

Setting texture coordinates

By default, `ofSpherePrimitive` sets texture coordinates so that a texture is wrapped onto a sphere using *cylindrical projection*, as shown in the following image:

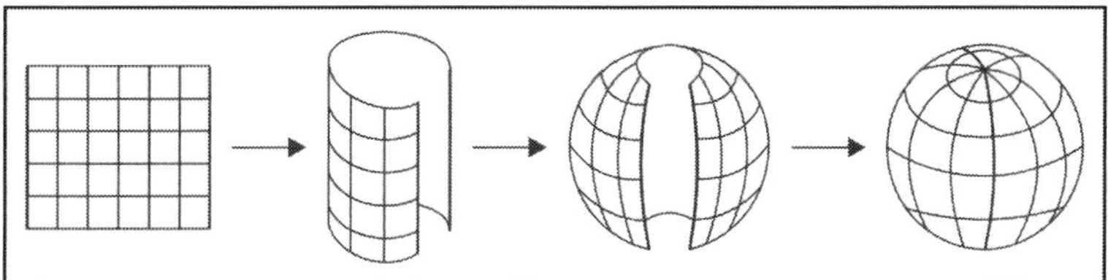

This shows the wrapping of texture on the sphere using cylindrical projection

This kind of projection is used in globes.

To set up the texture coordinates, we will use the `mapTexCoords(x0,y0,x1,y1)` method. The arguments `x0`, `y0`, `x1`, and `y1` denote the corners of the rectangular area inside the texture image, which should be used for wrapping.

As we want to use the whole picture of `fbo2` for texturing, we need to pass its dimensions to `mapTexCoords`. To achieve this, let's add the following code to `setup()`, after the `fbo2.allocate...` command:

```
float w = fbo2.getWidth();
float h = fbo2.getHeight();
sphere.mapTexCoords(0, h, w, 0);
sphere.rotate(180, 0, 1, 0);
```

The first and the second lines get dimensions of `fbo2` and put them into the variables `w` and `h`. The third line sets up corners of the area for texturing as `0`, `h` and `w`, and `0`. This is a rectangle covering the whole of `fbo2` but flipped vertically. Such flipping is required to negotiate flipping the *Y* axis that is imposed by the camera (see the *Creating a camera* section).

The last line isn't directly related to the texturing process, but it is needed to better orient the textured sphere. This line rotates the sphere at 180 degrees around the vector (`0, 1, 0`), that is, around the *Y* axis. As a result of rotation, the joint line of the wrapping will be put to the visible back of the sphere, and the center of the texture image will be put to the sphere's front.

Activating texturing

To texture a surface, we need to activate a texture using the texture's `bind` method before drawing and deactivate it after drawing using the texture's `unbind` method. Let's do it in the following way:

1. Activate the texture at the beginning of the `draw3d()` function:

   ```
   fbo2.getTextureReference().bind();
   ```

   All the drawing commands executed after this command will use the specified texture. In our example, such a drawing is only one command, `sphere.draw()`, so the sphere will be drawn textured with the `fbo2` image.

2. Deactivate the texture at the end of the `draw3d()` function:

   ```
   fbo2.getTextureReference().unbind();
   ```

Run the project and adjust the **image**, **video**, and other sliders. (If all the sliders are set to zero, the sphere will be drawn in black, and you will see nothing.) You will see a pretty nice textured sphere, as shown in the following screenshot:

This shows a textured sphere

You can try other sources of textures available in our project—image, video, or live image from video camera—by replacing `fbo2.getTextureReference()` in the previous code with the following variants, respectively:

```
image
video.getTextureReference()
camera.getTextureReference()
```

At this point, for the sake of video synthesis, it would be great to have an opportunity to mix up on the screen the *old* 2D image (stored now in `fbo2`) and the new 3D sphere. Let's implement such mixing by adding two GUI sliders.

Mixing 2D and 3D with the GUI

Let's create two sliders and use them to mix 2D and 3D graphics using the following steps:

1. Declare a new slider and a new offscreen buffer for storing the sphere image in the `ofApp` class:

   ```
   ofxFloatSlider show2d, show3d;
   ofFbo fbo3d;
   ```

2. Add commands to set up sliders and the offscreen buffer to `setup()`, after the `mixerGroup.add( ky.setup...` command:

   ```
   mixerGroup.add( show2d.setup("show2d", 255, 0, 255) );
   mixerGroup.add( show3d.setup("show3d", 255, 0, 255) );
   fbo3d.allocate( ofGetWidth(), ofGetHeight(), GL_RGBA );
   ```

   The first and second lines set sliders to have a range from `0` to `255` and add them to the GUI group `mixerGroup` (this group was created in the previous chapter). The third line allocates the offscreen buffer with size equal to the screen size. We set the `GL_RGBA` pixel format for this buffer, so it will hold the pixels colors together with the alpha channel. Such a format is required here to properly mix `fbo3d` contents with `fbo2` contents using the alpha blending mode.

3. Implement the mixing of 2D and 3D pictures by replacing the `draw3d()` command in the `draw()` function with the following code:

   ```
   fbo3d.begin();
   ofBackground( 0, 0 );
   draw3d();
   fbo3d.end();

   ofBackground( 0 );
   ofSetColor( 255, show2d );
   fbo2.draw( 0, 0 );
   ofSetColor( 255, show3d );
   fbo3d.draw( 0, 0 );
   ```

The code consists of two blocks. The first block draws the sphere to the `fbo3d` buffer. That is, the first line redirects drawing to the `fbo3d` buffer. The second line sets a black transparent background. The third line draws the sphere, and the last line redirects drawing back to the screen. As a result, the content of the buffer is a sphere drawn on a transparent background, so it is suited for layering using the alpha blending mode.

The second block sets a black background and then draws the contents of `fbo2` (layer with 2D) and `fbo3d` (layer with 3D) on the screen with transparency values depending on the sliders' `show2d` and `show3d` values.

On running the project, you will see a 2D image mixed with 3D sphere, as shown in this screenshot:

This is a 2D image mixed with 3D sphere image

Also, note the new sliders **show2d** and **show3d**. Adjust them to obtain different mixes of 2D and 3D layers.

Note that to have an opportunity to draw a sphere semitransparent, we use an additional offscreen buffer, `fbo3d`. The reason for such a trick is in fact that Z-buffering and blending do not work together properly in a simple way. (If we try drawing a sphere right on the screen using a semitransparent color, we will get notable drawing artifacts.)

The last topic we will consider is deforming the sphere's surface.

Deforming a sphere

Deformation, that is, changing the geometry of a surface, gives an opportunity to create new and unusual 3D shapes. We will explore two methods of deformation: shifting the sphere's vertices using analytical formulas and extruding the sphere's surface using a texture's pixels values.

To implement this, let's start with adding several sliders to control deformation in the following way:

1. Declare new sliders in the `ofApp` class:

   ```
   ofxFloatSlider rad, deform, deformFreq, extrude;
   ```

   This line declares four sliders: sphere radius, amount and frequency of analytical deformation, and amount of extrusion.

2. Add commands to set up sliders to `setup()` after the `mixerGroup.add( show3d.setup...` command:

   ```
   mixerGroup.add( rad.setup("rad", 250, 0, 500) );
   mixerGroup.add( deform.setup("deform", 0.3, 0, 1.5) );
   mixerGroup.add( deformFreq.setup("deformFreq", 3, 0, 10) );
   mixerGroup.add( extrude.setup("extrude", 1, 0, 1 ) );
   ```

Deforming by formulas

We will implement the sphere deformation by changing positions of its vertices in the `update()` function. To achieve this, perform the following steps:

1. Declare an array of 3D points in the `ofApp` class to store the original vertices' positions:

   ```
   vector<ofPoint> vertices0;
   ```

2. Copy the original sphere's vertices to the `vertices0` array by adding the following command after `sphere.set...` in `setup()`:

   ```
   vertices0 = sphere.getMesh().getVertices();
   ```

   Here, `sphere.getMesh()` returns the reference to the `ofMesh` object of the sphere, and that `getVertices()` returns the reference to the array (represented as `vector`) of the mesh's vertices. Finally, this array is copied to `vertices0`.

See the details on the `ofPoint` class in the *Introduction to 3D graphics with openFrameworks* section and a short description of the `ofMesh` class in the *openFrameworks classes for surface representation* section.

3. Change the positions of the sphere's vertices by adding the following code at the end of `update()`:

```
vector<ofPoint> &vertices = sphere.getMesh().getVertices();
for (int i=0; i<vertices.size(); i++) {
  ofPoint v = vertices0[i];
  v.normalize();
  float sx = sin( v.x * deformFreq );
  float sy = sin( v.y * deformFreq );
  float sz = sin( v.z * deformFreq );
  v.x += sy * sz * deform;
  v.y += sx * sz * deform;
  v.z += sx * sy * deform;
  v *= rad;
  vertices[i] = v;
}
```

The first line declares `vertices` as a reference to an array (because it is declared with `&`) and sets it to the current vertices' positions of the sphere to the `vertices` array. As this is a reference, no copying of data is performed, and also changing these array elements will change the vertices' positions of the sphere's mesh.

The next line performs a for-loop that runs `i` over all indices in the `vertices` array. The first line in the loop's block sets `v` as equal to the original position of the vertex with index `i`. The second line normalizes `v`, that is, sets it to the unit length. The next three lines' compute values `sx`, `sy`, and `sz`, which periodically (due to the use of the `sin` function) depend on the `x`, `y`, and `z` components of `v` and the `deformFreq` slider's value. The next three lines shift the components of `v` on values, depending on `sx`, `sy`, and `sz` and the `deform` slider's value.

Finally, the `v *= rad` command enlarges the length of `v` by `rad` times, and the `vertices[i] = v` command sets the sphere's vertex with index `i` equal to `v`.

> The idea behind this transformation of `v` was to create periodical shifting, with formulas symmetrical for all components `x`, `y`, and `z`. Feel free to experiment and change it on your own.

Run the project and change the **rad**, **deform**, and **deformFreq** sliders. You will find that **rad** sets the radius of the sphere, and **deform** and **deformFreq** control the amount and space frequency of deformation. The sphere will be deformed, as shown in the following screenshot:

This shows a deformed sphere

Note that we don't update normals, so normals keep their values as they are set for an undeformed sphere. Thus, for a deformed sphere, these values of normals are not exactly perpendicular to the surface, and so lighting is not perfect. Nevertheless, the result we obtained is pretty nice for our purposes.

Currently, openFrameworks does not have a unified way to update the normals of deformed surfaces (but see the `getFaceNormals` method of the `ofMesh` class to get a cue on how to do it). For such a purpose, we could recommend that you use the `setNormals` function, which is defined in example codes for our book *Mastering openFrameworks: Creative Coding Demystified*, published by Packt Publishing. These codes can be downloaded freely from `www.packtpub.com`.

The considered deformation method shifts vertices using formulas. Now, we will consider another type of deformation, called extruding, which shifts vertices based not on formulas, but on a picture's pixel values.

Extruding the sphere

Let's implement the **extruding** of the sphere using the brightness of the pixels of a texture stored in the `fbo2` buffer. That is, we will shift the vertices of the sphere radially; the value of the shifting will depend on the corresponding pixel's brightness in the texture.

> The effect we are developing here is similar to openFrameworks' example, `3d/meshFromCamera`, which we considered in the first chapter (in the *Running your first example* section). That example implemented the extruding of a plane by shifting the vertices perpendicular to the plane. Here, we will implement it for a sphere.

To accomplish this, perform the following steps:

1. Increase the resolution of the sphere by replacing the `sphere.set(250, 20)` in `setup()` command with:

   ```
   sphere.set(250, 80);
   ```

   Now the sphere will have `80` meridians and 80-1 = 79 parallels (and radius will remain at its old value, `250` pixels).

2. Insert the following code at the end of `update()`:

   ```
   ofPixels pixels;
   fbo2.readToPixels(pixels);

   for (int i=0; i<vertices.size(); i++) {
     ofVec2f t = sphere.getMesh().getTexCoords()[i];
     t.x = ofClamp( t.x, 0, pixels.getWidth()-1 );
     t.y = ofClamp( t.y, 0, pixels.getHeight()-1 );
     float br = pixels.getColor(t.x, t.y).getBrightness();
     vertices[i] *= 1 + br / 255.0 * extrude;
   }
   ```

The first line declares the pixel array `pixels` (see the *Raster images in openFrameworks* section in the previous chapter for details on the `ofPixels` class), and the second line reads the contents of the offscreen buffer `fbo2` to `pixels`.

The next line performs a for-loop, which runs `i` over all indices in the `vertices` array (`vertices` were declared in the previous section). The first line in the loop's block gets the texture coordinates `t` for a vertex with the index `i`. The type of `t` is `ofVec2f`; it's a two-dimensional vector (point) with float fields `x` and `y`. And `t` points out the place in the texture that is wrapped on the vertex with the index `i`.

In the second and third lines of the block, we clamp texture coordinates `t.x` and `t.y` to the dimensions of the pixel array `pixels`. (The necessity of this is in fact that the original `t.x` and `t.y` run a range of values, including maximal dimensions of the picture, and this maximal values goes out of the `pixels` array's dimensions).

In the fourth line, we get the brightness `br` of the color of the pixel (`t.x`, `t.y`) in `pixels`. In the last line, we enlarge the length of `vertices[i]` proportionally to `br` and the `extrude` slider's value (we defined this slider in the previous section).

Run the project and set the **deform** slider to zero to temporarily disable analytical deformations. You will see a beautiful 3D object, as shown in the following screenshot:

This is an example of an extruded sphere

> The screenshot was obtained using **extrude** equal to `1`, with the enabled kaleidoscope effect with **ksectors** equal to `5`.
>
> If you want to reproduce screenshots in this chapter in your project, load presets included in the archive with example codes for this book. (To load a preset, press *L* in the project).

This beautiful effect culminates our trip to 3D graphics and our development of the visual part of the video synthesizer project.

Summary

In this chapter, we considered the basics of 3D graphics. We looked at an example of drawing a sphere in 3D. We explored how to draw wireframe, solid, and textured sphere. Also, we considered deforming its shape by formulas and extruding. Besides that, you learned to use the camera object and implement the capability to mix a 3D picture layer with a 2D picture that we generated in previous chapters.

In the next chapter, we will explore a variety of ways to automate the project's parameters using timer, Perlin noise, sound, and neural data recordings, stored in a text file.

6
Animating Parameters

Most of the control parameters of our project are represented as GUI sliders. Until now, we adjusted them only manually using the mouse. In this chapter, we will discover several ways to automate sliders by covering the following topics:

- Using time values for a parameter's automation
- Using Perlin noise
- Playing an audio file, capturing the sound from a sound card, and measuring the sound level
- Reading and parsing data from a text file

At the end of the chapter, we will obtain a project that generates animated visuals, reacts on a prerecorded or captured level of sound, and reads a parameter's values from a text file containing neural data recording.

In our examples, we will consider the automation of GUI sliders only, because you can explicitly see how their values change by looking at the screen. Of course, the considered approach can be used to automate any parameters of the project, even if it is not represented as a slider.

Using time values for a parameter's automation

Using time values is apparently the most commonly used method to automate a parameter. In this approach, a parameter's value is set to be a function depending on the time, and more precisely, the number of seconds measured from some initial point in time.

Dependency of time can be implemented in many ways—as a mathematical expression, in tabular form, or even by drawing it using a graphics tablet. We will consider the simplest way, which is using mathematical expressions.

To implement dependency of time, we need a function to measure it. In openFrameworks, such a function is `ofGetElapsedTime()`. It returns the number of seconds elapsed from the project's start. This is a float value and is measured with millisecond precision.

To check this function, add the following command to the end of `update()`:

```
kangle = ofGetElapsedTimef();
```

This command sets the value of the **kangle** slider to the number of seconds elapsed from the project's start. On running the project, you will see how the **kangle** slider starts from zero and increases its value by one unit per second.

In the considered example, **kangle** depends on time in a linear fashion, and hence increases infinitely. But in many cases, we want parameter values to be bound by some fixed range. For such a purpose, a periodical function is often used. Let's consider this case now.

Implementing a simple LFO

Devices that create periodic changes in the parameters are widely used in sound and video synthesizers and are known as **Low Frequency Oscillators** (**LFOs**). We will implement a simple LFO that will control the `kx` slider using a sine wave.

The `kx` slider will fluctuate periodically in a range, say, from `0.45` to `0.55`, with a frequency of `0.1` Hz.

A frequency of `0.1` Hz means that we will get one period of fluctuation per $1 / 0.1 = 10$ *seconds.*

To achieve this, add the following code to the end of `update()`:

```
float phase = 0.1 * ofGetElapsedTimef() * M_TWO_PI;
float value = sin( phase );
kx = ofMap(value, -1, 1, 0.45, 0.55);
```

The first line computes the **instantaneous phase**; we multiply the frequency, `0.1`, by the time elapsed, `ofGetElapsedTimef()`, to obtain the number of cycles at a given point in time. Then, we multiply it by `M_TWO_PI`, which is a predefined constant equal to 2π. In this way, we obtain the number of cycles measured in radians (one cycle has a measure 2π or, equally, 360 degrees). As a result, we get the `phase` value, which is an angle in radians, describing our fluctuation at a given point in time.

The second line computes `value` by computing a value of the `sin()` function using `phase` as an argument. From the properties of the `sin()` function, it follows that it generates a sine wave, and `value` fluctuates with a frequency of `0.1` Hz in the range from `-1` to `1`.

The last line linearly maps `value` from the range [`-1, 1`] to the range [`0.45, 0.55`], so the resulting `kx` slider fluctuates from `0.45` to `0.55`, just as we need.

On running the project, you will see that the **kx** slider periodically fluctuates between `0.45` and `0.55`, and the full cycle of fluctuation takes 10 seconds.

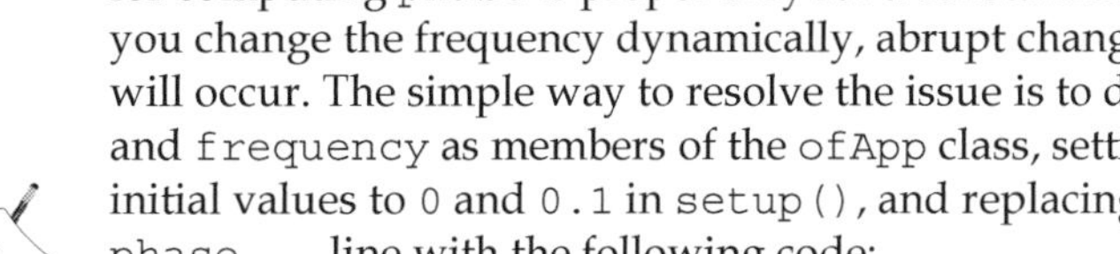

The described approach works well only if the frequency is constant during program execution. The reason is that the formula for computing `phase` is proper only for a constant frequency. So if you change the frequency dynamically, abrupt changes of `value` will occur. The simple way to resolve the issue is to declare `phase` and `frequency` as members of the `ofApp` class, setting their initial values to `0` and `0.1` in `setup()`, and replacing the `float phase...` line with the following code:

```
float dt = 1.0 / 60.0;
phase += dt * frequency * M_TWO_PI;
```

The first line defines the time step in seconds between two `update()` calls, and the second line updates the `phase` value. In this approach, you can change `frequency` in any way, for example, using a slider, and the `phase` value will change properly.

Now, we consider the implementation of the pseudorandom LFO using Perlin noise.

Implementing a pseudorandom LFO with Perlin noise

Perlin noise is a class of functions invented by Karl Perlin in 1983 to generate pseudorandom textures. The function of Perlin noise depends on one or several input values and returns a value, which continuously fluctuates in the range from `0` to `1`. The function is nonperiodical and looks like the realization of some random process. That is why it is called *noise*, but really, it's just a deterministic function with quite complex behavior.

Perlin noise is implemented in openFrameworks by the `ofNoise` function with overloaded variants that allows using one, two, three, or four input arguments, as follows:

```
ofNoise(x)
ofNoise(x,y)
ofNoise(x,y,z)
ofNoise(x,y,z,w)
```

Here, `x`, `y`, `z`, and `w` are input float values. Each function returns a float value from `0` to `1`, which continuously depends on input arguments and is quasiperiodic with the period `1` for each argument (that is, `ofNoise(x+1, y, z, w)` is similar, but in general, not equal to `ofNoise(x, y, z, w)`, and `ofNoise(x, y+1, z, w)` is similar, but in general, not equal to `ofNoise(x, y+1, z, w)`, and so on).

Strictly speaking, `ofNoise()` implements a modification of the original Perlin noise. It was developed by Karl Perlin in 2001 and is called **simplex noise**.

Perlin noise allows us to implement a pseudorandom LFO, that is, an LFO with pseudorandom behavior. To achieve this, add the following lines to the end of `update()` to automate the `deform` slider:

```
float phase1 = 0.2 * ofGetElapsedTimef();
deform = ofNoise( phase1 );
```

The first line computes `phase1`, which is a phase for Perlin noise with a frequency of `0.2` Hz. The second line computes Perlin noise using this phase and puts the result to the `deform` slider.

On running the project, you will see that **deform** fluctuates smoothly in quite an unpredictable way between `0` and `1`. Also, note that it possesses quasiperiodical behavior with a period length of *1 / 0.2 = 5 seconds*.

> To create the second pseudorandom LFO fluctuating with the same frequency, we cannot use `ofNoise( phase1 )` again, because it returns the same value as `deform` in the previous code. To resolve the problem, call the `ofNoise()` function with two arguments, such as the following:
>
> ```
> ofNoise( phase1, 29.81 )
> ```
>
> Here, the first argument is the phase again, and the second argument is some random number. In this case, the returned values will not correlate with the `ofNoise( phase1 )` values but will have a similar behavior. Using this approach, you can create as many LFOs as you need using `ofNoise` with different second arguments.

We considered how to create periodic and pseudorandom automation of parameters using time information. Now let's explore how to analyze sounds.

Using the level of sound for a parameter's automation

Real-time analysis of sound lets us create audio-reactive visuals. It is an important part of any video synthesizer. Here, we consider the simplest case of analysis—getting the level of sound and using it to control a parameter of our project.

We consider two ways of getting a sound: by playing an audio file and by capturing a sound from the sound card's input.

Playing and analyzing an audio file

openFrameworks has a powerful class for audio file playback, called `ofSoundPlayer`. It loads an audio file of various formats, including MP3, WAV, and AIFF, plays it, and controls its basic parameters, such as volume, pan, and speed.

Let's use this class to play an audio file by performing the following steps:

1. Add the audio player object definition to the `ofApp` class:

   ```
   ofSoundPlayer sound;
   ```

2. Load an audio file and set up its parameters by adding the following code to `setup()`:

   ```
   sound.loadSound( "skvo.wav" );
   sound.setVolume( 0.8 );
   sound.setLoop( true );
   ```

The first command loads the `skvo.wav` audio file from the `bin/data` folder of the project (we will copy this file there a little later). The second command sets the volume of the sound to `0.8`. It means that the sound will play at 80 percent of its original volume. The last command specifies that sound will play looped.

Other commands to control sound are:

- `sound.setMultiPlay(true)`: This command enables the mode for playing several instances of a sound. It is useful when programming the sound in games.
- `sound.setSpeed(0.5)`: This command sets the speed of the sound playing at 50 percent of its original speed, so the sound plays twice as long, and its pitch becomes lower by octave. Such a command is useful for programming a sound sampler.
- `sound.setPan(1)`: This command sets the stereo pan of the sound to the right channel. If the argument is equal to `-1`, the pan is set to the left channel. By default, the pan is set to zero, that is, the stereo panorama of the sound is not changed.

3. Start the sound to play and stop it by pressing *P* by adding the following code to `keyPressed()`:

```
if ( key == 'p' ) {
  if ( !sound.getIsPlaying() ) sound.play();
  else sound.stop();
}
```

   The first line checks whether the key pressed is *P*. The second line checks whether the sound is not playing and starts it to play. The third line executes only if the sound is playing and stops it.

4. Add a command to update openFrameworks' sound engine to the *beginning* of `update()` (we place this command in the beginning for separating it from the other code added in this chapter; it will be needed in the upcoming *Controlling automation* section):

```
ofSoundUpdate();
```

We should call this command regularly so that the `ofSoundPlayer` objects work properly. The simplest way to do it is calling this command in `update()`.

5. Finally, copy the `skvo.wav` audio file to the `bin/data` folder of the project. You can get the file from the archive provided with the book.

The `skvo.wav` music track is written by Leksha, `soundcloud.com/leksha`. With the consent of the author, this track can be used in creative projects without any restrictions.

Run the project and press *P*. The music track begins to play. Press *P* again to stop it.

Now let's measure the momentary level of this music track and use it to control the `rad` slider.

Getting the level of a sound signal

To get the level of a sound signal generated by `ofSoundPlayer` objects, we can use the `ofSoundGetSpectrum()` function. It returns a pointer on the *spectrum* values of a short part of the currently playing sound signal.

A **spectrum** is an array of amplitudes of *Fast Fourier Transform* coefficients for a given piece of a sound signal. It describes the amount of various frequencies presented in the sound (see *Frequency spectrum*, a Wikipedia article at `en.wikipedia.org/wiki/Frequency_spectrum`).

Strictly speaking, `ofSoundGetSpectrum()` returns only the first half of the spectrum values. The second half is symmetrical to the first half and doesn't give any new information about the sound signal.

Using spectrum, it is easy to estimate the level of sound using the **Root Mean Square (RMS)** measure. Let's implement it by adding the following code to the end of `update()`:

```
float *spectrum = ofSoundGetSpectrum(128);
double level = 0;
for (int i=0; i<128; i++) {
  level += spectrum[i] * spectrum[i];
}
level = sqrt( level / 128 );
```

The first line gets the `spectrum` array with a size of `128`. It is just a pointer to an array that is managed by openFrameworks' sound engine, so we don't need to free the memory after using it.

The second line declares the `level` variable, and the next three lines compute the sum of squares of all the `spectrum` values. The last line gets the square root of `level` divided by `128`, that is, by the number of `spectrum` elements. By definition, it is an RMS value of the spectrum, and it is an estimation of the sound level.

[To get a measure of the sound level in *decibels*, we need to get the logarithm from the `level` value. However, for simplicity, here we will use the linear value we already have.]

Now, let's apply the `level` value to automate the `rad` slider by adding the following lines to `update()`, right after the previous code:

```
float newRad = ofMap( level, 0, 1, 100, 200, true );
rad = rad + 0.1 * (newRad-rad);
```

The first line linearly maps the `level` value from the range [`0, 1`] to the range [`100, 200`] and puts the result to the `newRad` variable. The last argument `true` specifies that the output result will be truncated to the range [`100, 200`], even if `level` gets out of the range [`0, 1`].

The second moves the `rad` slider value to the `newRad` value smoothly. The constant `0.1` is a moving speed: in one step, `rad` moves by `0.1` of the distance between `rad` and `newRad`. This smoothing method is called **exponential smoothing**, and `0.1` is called the **smoothing factor**.

[For details on exponential smoothing, see Wikipedia's article at `en.wikipedia.org/wiki/Exponential_smoothing`. Note that there is another formula used for smoothing, which is equivalent to our formula. To show equivalence, let's expand the brackets in our formula and group the terms, as follows:

*rad + 0.1 * (newRad – rad) = rad + 0.1 * newRad – 0.1 * rad*
*= 0.1 * newRad + (1 – 0.1 * rad)*

We get the formula used in the article.]

Run the project and press *P*. The music begins to play, and you will see that the **rad** slider value follows the level of the sound.

Try to change the smoothing factor from `0.1` to other values (in the range from `0` to `1`). Using a lower value (for example, `0.05`) results in more smoothing, and using a larger value (for example, `0.2`) results in less smoothing but better responsiveness.

We just implemented processing a prerecorded audio track. This technique can be used to create visuals for shows and performances when the audio track is fixed. But for situations where music is played by live musicians, we need to capture the analyzed sound from the sound card's input. Let's consider it.

Capturing sound from a sound card's input and measuring its level

openFrameworks has an opportunity to capture live sound from a sound card's input, such as a microphone or a line input.

> The code in this section will work properly only if your computer has a sound input. Most probably, your laptop already has a built-in microphone. If your computer has no sound input, you can use an external sound card connected via USB or any other type of connection.

To enable sound capture and measure its level, perform the following steps:

1. Add the declarations of a new function and a variable to the `ofApp` class:

   ```
   void audioIn(float *input, int bufferSize, int nChannels);
   float soundLevel;
   ```

   The first line declares the `audioIn()` function, which will be called by openFrameworks when a new part of an input sound has arrived from a sound card. We will consider its arguments in the next step. The second line defines a variable, `soundLevel`, which will store the current sound level value.

2. Initialize the `soundLevel` variable and start to capture the sound by adding the following lines to `setup()`:

   ```
   soundLevel = 0;
   ofSoundStreamSetup( 0, 1, 44100, 128, 4 );
   ```

   The first line just sets `soundLevel` to zero. The second line starts capturing the input sound to our program. The first and second arguments of the `ofSoundStreamSetup()` function specify the number of output and input channels. We need no output channels and only one input channel (mono input), so they are `0` and `1` respectively.

The third argument is a **sample rate** of the sound stream, that is, the number of measures of the sound (called **sound samples**) per second. We use the value `44100` for it. It is quite a generic value that corresponds to the quality of compact disc recording. The fourth argument is the size of the sound buffer, that is, the number of sound samples on which the input sound stream is separated and sent to our program.

The last argument is a number of sound buffers used by the sound card to protect the sound buffer from overloading. We use the generic value `4`.

With our settings, the sound buffer stores $128 / 44100 \approx 0.0029$ seconds of sound, and we need to process `44100 / 128 ≈ 345` of such buffers per second.

3. Add the definition of the `audioIn()` function to the `ofApp.cpp` file:

```
void ofApp::audioIn(float *input, int bufferSize,
  int nChannels){
  double v = 0;
  for (int i=0; i<bufferSize; i++) {
    v += input[i] * input[i];
  }
  v = sqrt( v / bufferSize );
  soundLevel = v;
}
```

This function will be called by openFrameworks when the sound card accumulates a sound buffer for processing. The `input` parameter is an input buffer array, `bufferSize` is the size of the input buffer, and `nChannels` is the number of input sound channels. The first lines of the function compute the RMS value of the input buffer and write its value to the `v` variable.

The last line writes the computed value to the `soundLevel` variable, which we will use in `update()`.

This code to compute the RMS value is similar to the code described in the previous *Getting the level of a sound signal* section of this chapter. The one important difference here is that `input` is an array of sound samples but not a spectrum array as it was in the previous code. However, following *Parseval's theorem*, computing RMS using both approaches, spectrum and samples, gives equal values. So both approaches (computing RMS from the spectrum and from the sound samples) give similar results.

4. Finally, let's use the computed `soundLevel` value to adjust the `rad` slider. Add the following line to `update()` before the `float newRad = ofMap...` command:

   ```
   level += soundLevel;
   ```

   This command increases the `level` variable by the `soundLevel` value. Now, `level` is the sum of the level of a played audio file and the level of the captured sound. So, the `rad` slider reacts on both sound sources.

On running the project and giving some sound to a microphone (or line input), you will notice that the **rad** slider jumps accordingly.

We considered getting data from sounds. Now, we will implement reading data from text files with an example of parsing neural data.

Reading data from a text file

A fruitful source of input data for parameter automation are text files. Such files can contain various pieces of information, such as statistics of the weather (temperature) for a century, solar activity forecast, or recordings of human body motion captured by depth cameras. By parsing data from these files and using it as values for a project's parameters, we can obtain quite an interesting (and scientifically meaningful) parameter's automation.

Let's demonstrate it by parsing the `eeg.txt` text file containing a 128-channel **electroencephalography** (EEG) recording. This file is contained in the archive provided with the book.

The EEG recording file, `eeg.txt`, was made by the Laboratory for Brain and Neurocognitive Development, Ural Federal University, Ekaterinburg, Russia. With the consent of the laboratory, this recording can be used as a source of input data in creative projects without any restrictions. For recording, *HydroCel Geodesic Sensor Net* from Electrical Geodesics, Inc. was used.

openFrameworks contains the `ofFile` and `ofBuffer` classes, which are intended to work with files and read their contents. To use them to read the text file, perform the following steps:

1. Add the declarations of a file and a buffer for the file reading to the `ofApp` class, as follows:

   ```
   ofFile file;
   ofBuffer buffer;
   ```

2. Open a file and prepare a buffer object to read data from the file by adding the following commands to `setup()`:

   ```
   file.open("eeg.txt");
   buffer.set(file);
   ```

   The first line opens the `bin/data/eeg.txt` file for reading, and the second line sets a buffer object to be ready to read data from this file.

3. Add the following commands to the end of `update()` to read a line from the file and use it to control the `twistX` and `twistY` sliders:

   ```
   if ( buffer.isLastLine() ) buffer.resetLineReader();
   string line = buffer.getNextLine();
   vector<string> values = ofSplitString( line, "\t" );
   if ( values.size() >= 128 ) {
     float value1 = ofToFloat(values[1]);
     float value2 = ofToFloat(values[5]);
     float value3 = ofToFloat(values[100]);
     twistX = ofMap( value2-value1, -9400, -9100, -10, 10 );
     twistY = ofMap( value3-value1, -1700, -1650, -10, 10 );
   }
   ```

   The first line checks whether we read the last line in the file, and if so, it restarts reading from the beginning. The second line reads the line from the file to the `line` string.

   The third line splits `line` into an array of `values` strings using the *Tab* symbol (`"\t"`) as a delimiter. The reason for this is that each line in `eeg.txt` contains 129 numbers, separated by *Tab*. The first 128 numbers are values obtained from the 128 channels, measured in microvolts. The last number is equal to zero.

   So, we can use the first 128 values for our parameter's automation. In the fourth line, we verify that values array has a size not less than 128 (it is a good idea to check this to make sure we are reading a proper file). Then, in the next three lines, we convert values from the channels `2` (`1` + `1`), `6` (`5` + `1`), and `101` (`100` + `1`) (in an array, indices begin with zero) into float numbers `value1`, `value2`, and `value3` respectively. The last two lines use the difference between these numbers to set values to the `twistX` and `twistY` sliders.

4. Finally, copy the `eeg.txt` file to the `bin/data` folder of the project. You can get the file from the archive provided with the book.

On running the project, you will see that the **twistX** and **twistY** sliders fluctuate; they appear according to the values read from the file.

The original recording was made with a speed of 1,000 lines per second. Our project reads one line per `update()` calling, that is, 60 lines per second. Hence, the speed we playback the data at is $1000 / 60 \approx 17$ times slower than the speed of recording.

Note that we selected the channels and formulas to animate `twistX` and `twistY` empirically, with an aim to obtain spectacular pulsating visuals, as shown in this screenshot:

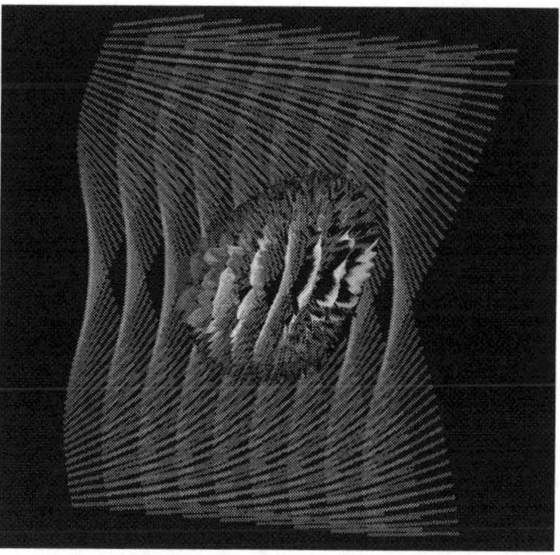

This shows the EEG data visualization

If you want to reproduce this screenshot in your project, please load a preset for this chapter, included in the archive with the example code for this book. (To load a preset, press *L* in the project).

So, feel free to explore other channels and formulas on your own!

Controlling automation

At this point, we have implemented automation for several sliders. Often, it is desirable to have an opportunity to disable automation. So let's add a checkbox that toggles automation on and off:

1. Declare a new checkbox in the `ofApp` class:

   ```
   ofxToggle automate;
   ```

2. Set up the checkbox in `setup()` by inserting the following command after the `mixerGroup.add( extrude.setup...` command:

   ```
   mixerGroup.add( automate.setup( "automate", true ) );
   ```

3. Insert the following line right before all the code we added in this chapter to `update()` (except the `ofSoundUpdate()` command, which we placed at the beginning of the function):

   ```
   if ( automate ) {
   ```

   And insert the following line right after that code:

   ```
   }
   ```

> You need to re-indent that code by adding *Tab* before each line to have proper indentation.

Now, automation will work only if the `automate` checkbox is checked. In the same way, you can create separate checkboxes to toggle the automation of each parameter we created.

Also, you can create sliders for the control parameters of LFOs (such as frequency and range of output) and for other automation algorithms discussed in this chapter.

Summary

In this chapter, we considered several sources of data to animate parameters of the project. At first, we implemented time-dependent LFO and Perlin noise. Then, we explored how to play and capture sounds and measure the level of sound using RMS measure. Finally, you learned to read lines from a text file, parse them, and use them for a parameter's automation.

The data sources we explored can be named *built-in* sources, because they rely on capabilities that are built into the computer itself. In the next chapter, we will study using *external* data sources, such as controlling the project by networking and connecting new peripheral devices using the Arduino board.

7
Distributed and Physical Computing with Networking and Arduino

Until now, we have created a single openFrameworks project that works on a single computer. In this chapter, we will investigate how to create a distributed project consisting of several programs working together and communicating with each other via networking. Also, we will consider how to use an Arduino board to get data from various electronic inputs, such as potentiometers. In this chapter, we will cover the following topics:

- Networking in openFrameworks
- Receiving and sending OSC data in openFrameworks
- Creating OSC sender for a mobile device using the TouchOSC app
- Creating OSC senders in Python and Max/MSP
- Receiving data from an Arduino board

[Along the chapter, we will use networking and Arduino data to adjust just one GUI slider, `pinchY`. Of course, you can use such data to adjust any other GUI sliders and arbitrary variables of your project.]

Distributed computing with networking

Networking is a way of sending and receiving data between programs, which work on a single or different computers and mobile devices. Using networking, it is possible to split a complex project into several programs working together.

There are at least three reasons to create distributed projects:

- The first reason is splitting to obtain better performance. For example, when creating a big interactive wall with cameras and projectors, it is possible to use two computers. The first computer (*tracker*) will process data from cameras and send the result to the second computer (*render*), which will render the picture and output it to projectors.
- The second reason is creating a heterogeneous project using different development languages. For example, consider a project that generates a real-time visualization of data captured from the Web. It is easy to capture and analyze the data from the Web using a programming language like Python, but it is hard to create a rich, real-time visualization with it.

  On the opposite side, openFrameworks is good for real-time visualization but is not very elegant when dealing with data from the Web. So, it is a good idea to build a project consisting of two programs. The first Python program will capture data from the Web, and the second openFrameworks program will perform rendering.
- The third reason is synchronization with, and external control of, one program with other programs/devices. For example, a video synthesizer can be controlled from other computers and mobiles via networking. We will consider this case in the chapter in detail.

Networking in openFrameworks

openFrameworks' networking capabilities are implemented in two core addons: `ofxNetwork` and `ofxOsc`.

> To use an addon in your project, you need to include it in the new project when creating a project using Project Generator (see *Chapter 2, Creating Your First openFrameworks Project*), or by including the addon's headers and libraries into the existing project manually. If you need to use only one particular addon, you can use an existing addon's example as a sketch for your project.
>
> We have already included the `ofxOsc` addon in our `VideoSynth` project while creating it in *Chapter 2, Creating Your First openFrameworks Project*.

The ofxNetwork addon

The `ofxNetwork` addon contains classes for sending and receiving data using the **Transmission Control Protocol** (**TCP**) and the **User Datagram Protocol** (**UDP**). The difference between these protocols is that TCP guarantees receiving data without losses and errors but requires the establishment of a preliminary connection (known as **handshake**) between a sender and a receiver. UDP doesn't require the establishment of any preliminary connection but also doesn't guarantee delivery and correctness of the received data.

Typically, TCP is used in tasks where data needs to be received without errors, such as downloading a JPEG file from a web server. UDP is used in tasks where data should be received in real time at a fast rate, such as receiving a game state 60 times per second in a networking game.

The `ofxNetwork` addon's classes are quite generic and allow the implementation of a wide range of low-level networking tasks. In the book, we don't explore it in detail. For more information, see the `networkTcpClientExample`, `networkTcpServerExample`, `networkUdpReceiverExample`, and `networkUdpSenderExample` examples, which are placed in openFrameworks' `examples/addons` folder.

The ofxOsc addon

The `ofxOsc` addon is intended for sending and receiving messages using the **Open Sound Control** (**OSC**) protocol. Messages of this protocol (OSC messages) are intended to store control commands and parameter values.

This protocol is very popular today and is implemented in many VJ and multimedia programs and software for live electronic sound performance. All the popular programming tools support OSC too.

An OSC protocol can use the UDP or TCP protocols for data transmission. Most often, as in openFrameworks implementation, a UDP protocol is used. See details of the OSC protocol at `opensoundcontrol.org/spec-1_0`.

The main classes of `ofxOsc` are the following:

- `ofxOscSender`: This sends OSC messages
- `ofxOscReceiver`: This receives OSC messages
- `ofxOscMessage`: This class is for storing a single OSC message
- `ofxOscBundle`: This class is for storing several OSC messages, which can be sent and received as a bundle

Let's add the OSC receiver to our `VideoSynth` project and then create a simple OSC sender, which will send messages to the `VideoSynth` project.

Implementing the OSC messages receiver

To implement the receiving of OSC messages in the `VideoSynth` project, perform the following steps:

1. Include the `ofxOsc` addon's header to the `ofApp.h` file by inserting the following line after the `#include "ofxGui.h"` line:

   ```
   #include "ofxOsc.h"
   ```

2. Add a declaration of the OSC receiver object to the `ofApp` class:

   ```
   ofxOscReceiver oscReceiver;
   ```

3. Set up the OSC receiver in `setup()`:

   ```
   oscReceiver.setup( 12345 );
   ```

   The argument of the `setup()` method is the networking port number. After executing this command, `oscReceiver` begins listening on this port for incoming OSC messages. Each received message is added to a special message queue for further processing.

A **networking port** is a number from 0 to 65535. Ports from 10000 to 65535 normally are not used by existing operating systems, so you can use them as port numbers for OSC messages. Note that two programs receiving networking data and working on the same computer must have different port numbers.

4. Add the processing of incoming OSC messages to `update()`:

   ```
   while ( oscReceiver.hasWaitingMessages() ) {
     ofxOscMessage m;
     oscReceiver.getNextMessage( &m );
     if ( m.getAddress() == "/pinchY" ) {
       pinchY = m.getArgAsFloat( 0 );
     }
   }
   ```

The first line is a `while` loop, which checks whether there are unprocessed messages in the message queue of `oscReceiver`. The second line declares an empty OSC message `m`. The third line pops the latest message from the message queue and copies it to `m`. Now, we can process this message.

Any OSC message consists of two parts: an **address** and (optionally) one or several **arguments**. An address is a string beginning with the / character. An address denotes the name of a control command or the name of a parameter that should be adjusted. Arguments can be float, integer, or string values, which specify some parameters of the command.

In our example, we want to adjust the `pinchY` slider with OSC commands, so we expect to have an OSC message with the address `/pinchY` and the first argument with its float value. Hence, in the fourth line, we check whether the address of the `m` message is equal to `/pinchY`. If this is true, in the fifth line, we get the first message's argument (an argument with the index value `0`) and set the `pinchY` slider to this value.

Of course, we could use any other address instead of `/pinchY` (for example, `/val`), but normally, it is convenient to have the address similar to the parameter's name.

It is easy to control other sliders with OSC. For example, to add control of the `extrude` slider, just add the following code:

```
if ( m.getAddress() == "/extrude" ) {
  extrude = m.getArgAsFloat( 0 );
}
```

After running the project, nothing new happens; it works as always. But now, the project is listening for incoming OSC messages on port `12345`. To check this, let's create a tiny openFrameworks project that sends OSC messages.

Creating an OSC sender with openFrameworks

Let's create a new project `OscOF`, one that contains a GUI panel with one slider, and send the slider's value via OSC to the `VideoSynth` project.

Here, we assume that the OSC sender and receiver run on the same computer. See the details on running the sender on a separate computer in the upcoming *Sending OSC messages between two separate computers* section.

Now perform the following steps:

1. Create a new project using Project Generator. Namely, start Project Generator, set the project's name to `OscOF` (that means OSC with openFrameworks), and include the `ofxGui` and `ofxOsc` addons to the newly created project (see the details on using Project Generator in *Chapter 2, Creating Your First openFrameworks Project*). The `ofxGui` addon is needed to create the GUI slider, and the `ofxOsc` addon is needed to send OSC messages.
2. Open this project in your IDE.
3. Include both addons' headers to the `ofApp.h` file by inserting the following lines (after the `#include "ofMain.h"` line):

```
#include "ofxGui.h"
#include "ofxOsc.h"
```

4. Add the declarations of the OSC sender object, the GUI panel, and the GUI slider to the `ofApp` class declaration:

```
    ofxOscSender oscSender;
    ofxPanel gui;
    ofxFloatSlider slider;
    void sliderChanged( float &value );
```

The last line declares a new function, which will be called by openFrameworks when the slider's value is changed. This function will send the corresponding OSC message. The symbol `&` before `value` means that the `value` argument is passed to the function as a **reference**.

Using reference here is not important for us, but is required by `ofxGui`; please see the information on the notion of a reference in the C++ documentation.

5. Set up the OSC sender, the GUI panel with the slider, and the project's window title and size by adding the following code to `setup()`:

```
oscSender.setup( "localhost", 12345 );
slider.addListener( this, &ofApp::sliderChanged );
gui.setup( "Parameters" );
gui.add( slider.setup("pinchY", 0, 0, 1) );
ofSetWindowTitle( "OscOF" );
ofSetWindowShape( 300, 150 );
```

The first line starts the OSC sender. Here, the first argument specifies the IP address to which the OSC sender will send its messages. In our case, it is `"localhost"`. This means the sender will send data to the same computer on which the sender runs. The second argument specifies the networking port, `12345`. The difference between setting up the OSC sender and receiver is that we need to specify the address and port for the sender, and not only the port. Also, after starting, the sender does nothing until we give it the explicit command to send an OSC message.

The second line starts listening to the slider's value changes. The first and second arguments of the `addListener()` command specify the object (`this`) and its member function (`sliderChanged`), which should be called when the slider is changed.

The remaining lines set up the GUI panel, the GUI slider, and the project's window title and shape; these were discussed in detail in *Chapter 2, Creating Your First openFrameworks Project* and *Chapter 3, Adding a GUI and Handling Keyboard Events*.

6. Now, add the `sliderChanged()` function definition to `ofApp.cpp`:

```
void ofApp::sliderChanged( float &value ) {
  ofxOscMessage m;
  m.setAddress( "/pinchY" );
  m.addFloatArg( value );
  oscSender.sendMessage( m );
}
```

This function is called when the `slider` value is changed, and the `value` parameter is its new value. The first three lines of the function create an OSC message `m`, set its address to `/pinchY`, and add a float argument equal to `value`. The last line sends this OSC message.

As you may see, the `m` message's address (`/pinchY`) coincides with the address implemented in the previous section, which is expected by the receiver. Also, the receiver expects that this message has a float argument—and it is true too! So, the receiver will properly interpret our messages and set its `pinchY` slider to the desired value.

7. Finally, add the command to draw GUI to `draw()`:

```
gui.draw();
```

On running the project, you will see its window, consisting of a GUI panel with a slider, as shown in the following screenshot:

This is the OSC sender made with openFrameworks

Don't stop this project for a while. Run the `VideoSynth` project and change the **pinchY** slider's value in the **OscOF** window using the mouse. The `pinchY` slider in `VideoSynth` should change accordingly. This means that the OSC transmission between the two openFrameworks programs works.

If you are not interested in sending data between two separate computers, feel free to skip the following section.

Sending OSC messages between two separate computers

We have checked passing OSC messages between two programs that run on the same computer. Now let's consider a situation when an OSC sender and an OSC receiver run on two separate computers connected to the same **Local Area Network** (**LAN**) using Ethernet or Wi-Fi.

If you have two laptops, most probably they are already connected to the same networking router and hence are in the same LAN.

To make an OSC connection work in this case, we need to change the `"localhost"` value in the sender's setup command by the local IP address of the receiver's computer.

Typically, this address has a form like `"192.168.0.2"`, or it could be a name, for example, `"LAPTOP3"`.

You can get the receiver's computer IP address by opening the properties of your network adapter or by executing the `ifconfig` command in the terminal window (for OS X or Linux) or `ipconfig` in the command prompt window (for Windows).

Connection troubleshooting

If you set the IP address in the sender's setup, but OSC messages from the OSC sender don't come to the OSC receiver, then it could be caused by the network firewall or antivirus software, which blocks transmitting data over our `12345` port. So please check the firewall and antivirus settings.

To make sure that the connection between the two computers exists, use the `ping` command in the terminal (or the command prompt) window.

Creating OSC senders with TouchOSC, Python, and Max/MSP

At this point, we create the OSC sender using openFrameworks and send its data out to the `VideoSynth` project. But, it's easy to create the OSC sender using other programming tools. Such an opportunity can be useful for you in creating complex projects.

So, let's show how to create an OSC sender on a mobile device using the TouchOSC app and also create simple senders using the Python and Max/MSP languages.

If you are not interested in sending OSC from mobile devices or in Python or Max/MSP, feel free to skip the corresponding sections.

Creating an OSC sender for a mobile device using the TouchOSC app

It is very handy to control your openFrameworks project by a mobile device (or devices) using the OSC protocol.

You can create a custom OSC sender by yourself (see the next chapter, where we explain creating openFrameworks projects for mobiles), or you can use special apps made for this purpose.

One such application is **TouchOSC**. It's a paid application available for iOS (see `hexler.net/software/touchosc`) and Android (see `hexler.net/software/touchosc-android`).

Working with TouchOSC consists of four steps: creating the GUI panel (called **layout**) on the laptop, uploading it to a mobile device, setting up the OSC receiver's address and port, and working with the layout. Let's consider them in detail:

1. To create the layout, download, unzip, and run a special program, **TouchOSC Editor**, on a laptop (it's available for OS X, Windows, and Linux). Add the desired GUI elements on the layout by right-clicking on the layout.
2. When the layout is ready, upload it to a mobile device by running the TouchOSC app on the mobile and pressing the **Sync** button in TouchOSC Editor.
3. In the TouchOSC app, go to the settings and set up the OSC receiver's IP address and port number. Next, open the created layout by choosing it from the list of all the existing layouts.
4. Now, you can use the layout's GUI elements to send the OSC messages to your openFrameworks project (and, of course, to any other OSC-supporting software).

Creating an OSC sender with Python

In this section, we will create a project that sends OSC messages using the Python language.

Here, we assume that the OSC sender and receiver run on the same computer. See the details on running the sender on a separate computer in the previous *Sending OSC messages between two separate computers* section.

Python is a free, interpreted language available for all operating systems. It is extremely popular nowadays in various fields, including teaching programming, developing web projects, and performing computations in natural sciences.

Using Python, you can easily capture information from the Web and social networks (using their API) and send it to openFrameworks for further processing, such as **visualization** or **sonification**, that is, converting data to a picture or sound.

Using Python, it is quite easy to create GUI applications, but here we consider creating a project without a GUI.

Perform the following steps to install Python, create an OSC sender, and run it:

1. Install Python from `www.python.org/downloads` (the current version is 3.4).
2. Download the `python-osc` library from `pypi.python.org/pypi/python-osc` and unzip it. This library implements the OSC protocol support in Python.
3. Install this library, open the terminal (or command prompt) window, go to the folder where you unzipped `python-osc` and type the following:

   ```
   python setup.py install
   ```

   If this doesn't work, type the following:

   ```
   python3 setup.py install
   ```

   Python is ready to send OSC messages. Now let's create the sender program.

4. Using your preferred code or text editor, create the `OscPython.py` file and fill it with the following code:

   ```
   from pythonosc import udp_client
   from pythonosc import osc_message_builder
   import time

   if __name__ == "__main__":
     oscSender = udp_client.UDPClient("localhost", 12345)
     for i in range(10):
       m = osc_message_builder.OscMessageBuilder(address =
         "/pinchY")
       m.add_arg(i*0.1)
       oscSender.send(m.build())
       print(i)
       time.sleep(1)
   ```

   The first three lines import the `udp_client`, `osc_message_builder`, and `time` modules for sending the UDP data (we will send OSC messages using UDP), creating OSC messages, and working with time respectively.

   The `if __name__ == "__main__":` line is generic for Python programs and denotes the part of the code that will be executed when the program runs from the command line.

   The first line of the executed code creates the `oscSender` object, which will send the UDP data to the `localhost` IP address and the `12345` port. The second line starts a `for` cycle, where `i` runs the values `0, 1, 2, …, 9`.

   The body of the cycle consists of commands for creating an OSC message `m` with address `/pinchY` and argument `i*0.1`, and sending it by OSC. The last two lines print the value `i` to the console and delay the execution for one second.

5. Open the terminal (or command prompt) window, go to the folder with the `OscPython.py` file, and execute it by the `python OscPython.py` command. If this doesn't work, use the `python3 OscPython.py` command.

The program starts and will send 10 OSC messages with the `/pinchY` address and the `0.0`, `0.1`, `0.2`, ..., `0.9` argument values, with 1 second of pause between the sent messages. Additionally, the program prints values from `0` to `9`, as shown in the following screenshot:

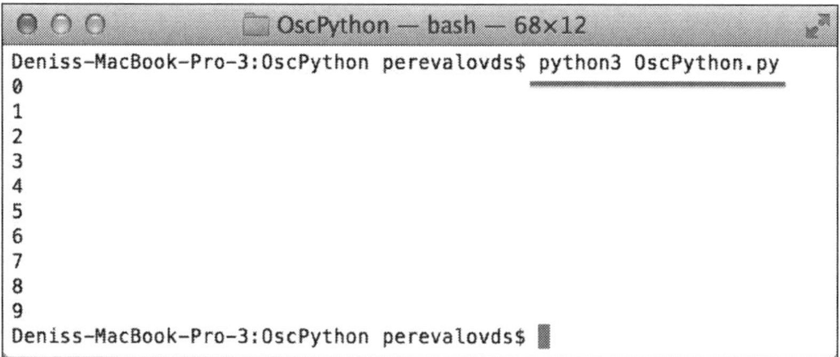

This is the output of an OSC sender made with Python

Run the `VideoSynth` project and start our Python sender again. You will see how its **pinchY** slider gradually changes from `0.0` to `0.9`. This means that OSC transmission from a Python program to an openFrameworks program works.

Creating an OSC sender with Max/MSP

In this section, we will create a project that sends OSC messages using the Max/MSP language.

In this section, we assume that the OSC sender and receiver runs on the same computer. See the details on running the sender on a separate computer in the previous *Sending OSC messages between two separate computers* section.

Max/MSP (whose full name is **Max/MSP/Jitter/Gen**) is a popular visual programming language and IDE used for interactive sound and multimedia programming.

Max/MSP is paid and available for OS X and Windows only. If you are working on Linux, or want to use a free software, please check Max/MSP's free analogue *Pure Data*, which is available for Linux, OS X, and Windows.

Though Max/MSP is paid, it has a fully functional free trial for 30 days. Also, it has free runtime, so you can deploy the developed programs on any number of computers freely.

Using Max/MSP, it is possible to create a GUI with dozens of parameters rapidly, create complex dependencies between parameters, and store a parameter's values into presets. Also, most sound and VJ USB controllers can be easily connected to Max/MSP as MIDI devices. So, you can use Max/MSP as a powerful super-controller, which collects and transforms data from all your MIDI-controllers and sends it to your openFrameworks project.

To install Max/MSP and create a simple OSC sender, perform the following steps:

1. Download Max/MSP from `cycling74.com/downloads` (the current version is 7.01).
2. Install and run it.
3. Go to the **File** menu and click on the **New Patcher...** item. A new window with an empty patch (that is, a Max/MSP program) will be created.
4. Now, let's create a slider object. Move the mouse inside the patch's window and press *N*. An empty text field will appear in the mouse position, as shown in the following screenshot:

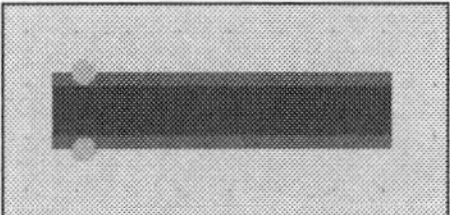

This is an empty text field

5. Type `slider` in the empty text field, as shown here:

This is the text field filled with slider text

6. Press *Return* (*Enter*). The text field turns into a slider, as shown in this screenshot:

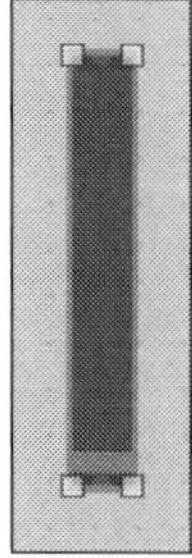

This is the created slider

7. Using the same approach, create four new objects by pressing *N* and typing the following commands:

```
/ 127.
flonum
/pinchY $1
udpsend localhost 12345
```

As a result, you will have five objects, as shown in the following screenshot:

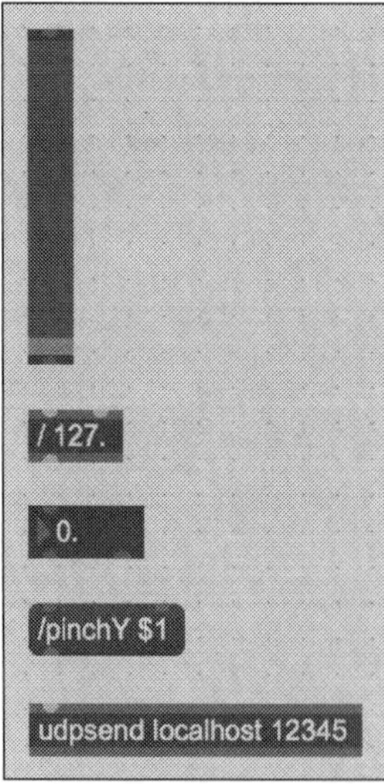

These are all objects of our Max/MSP patch

We will discuss the meaning of each object a little later. Now let's finish creating the patch.

Each Max/MSP object can have one or several inputs (**inlets**) located at its top, and one or several outputs (**outlets**) located at its bottom. Outlets can be connected with inlets by dragging the mouse. Such a connection is called **patch cord**, and it passes Max/MSP messages, sounds, or images between objects. In our case, all the patch cords pass messages.

8. Connect the left outlet of each from the first four objects with the left inlet of the succeeding object, as shown in this screenshot:

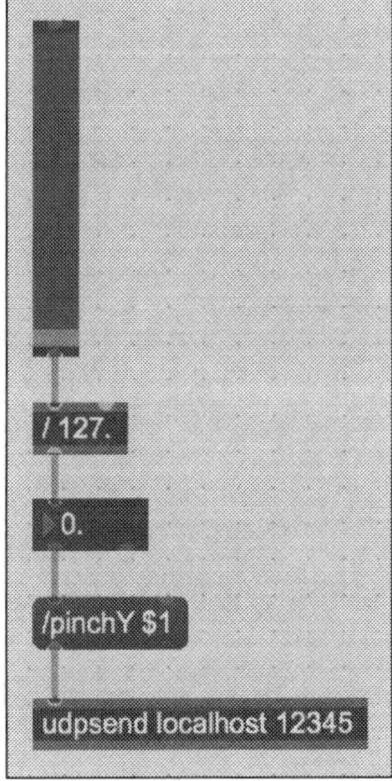

This is a ready Max/MSP patch sending OSC messages

The patch is ready!

The patch starts to execute immediately during its creation, so it is already executing. But, currently we can't adjust the slider's value by mouse because the slider is in editing mode and will move itself inside the patch. To be able to adjust the slider's value, we need to *lock the patch*, that is, disable its editing mode and enable adjusting the object's values.

9. Lock the patch by pressing *Command* + *E* (for OS X) or *Ctrl* + *E* (for Windows). Now you can adjust the slider's value using the mouse, and the corresponding values from `0` to `1` will be sent to the OSC receiver by OSC.

Run the `VideoSynth` project and check that its **pinchY** slider changes accordingly with the patch's slider value. This means that OSC transmission from a Max/MSP patch to an openFrameworks program works.

Now let's see what happens in the patch in detail:

- When we change the slider's value using the mouse, it sends an integer value from `0` to `127` to its outlet.
- The `/ 127.` object divides this value by `127` (the dot after number `127` means that division is performed using float arithmetic) and sends the resulting float value (which is from `0` to `1`) to the `flonum` object.
- The `flonum` object displays the received float value and also passes it to its left outlet.
- The `/pinchY $1` object constructs a string such as `/pinch 0.33` by replacing `$1` with the input value, and outputs the string to its outlet.
- The last object, `udpsend localhost 12345`, sends this string to the `localhost` IP address by UDP using port `12345`. The string will be interpreted by the OSC receiver as a proper OSC message with a `/pinchY` address and one float argument.

If you want to continue editing the patch, unlock it by pressing *Command* + *E* or *Ctrl* + *E* again.

In a similar way, you can create other sliders and connect all of them to the existing `udpsend` object.

In our patch, for simplicity, we used the slider's default range from `0` to `127`. But it is possible to change the slider's range to any values you want, including float-valued ranges. To do this, move the mouse pointer to a slider, right-click on the mouse, and in the context menu that appears, click on **Inspector**. You will see the properties page of the slider. The **Value** tab controls the slider's range, so you can change it as you need.

We have investigated enough to be able to create a distributed project containing several programs communicating with each other via the OSC protocol. Now let's consider physical computing with the Arduino board.

Physical computing with Arduino

Physical computing is a field related to modern **Do It Yourself** (**DIY**) and art projects. It is based on using sensors and various electromechanical devices together with computers and microcontrollers to create interactive physical systems, such as interactive installations and experimental toys.

Arduino is a popular open source physical computing platform consisting of a microcontroller board, an IDE, and a language for the board's programming. The Arduino IDE is available for OS X, Windows, and Linux.

In this section, we will consider how to read data from an analog input of the Arduino board and send it to our `VideoSynth` openFrameworks project.

To run the example in this section, you need an Arduino board. We will use here the Arduino Uno (Revision 3) board, but you can use any other one.

We begin with programming Arduino board and then change the `VideoSynth` project so it will read the Arduino data.

Programming an Arduino board

Let's start with the following steps:

1. Download the Arduino IDE from `www.arduino.cc` (the current version is 1.0.6).
2. Unzip and run it.
3. Go to the **File** menu and click on **New**. A new window with an empty **sketch** (that is, an Arduino program) will be created.
4. Fill it with the following code:

```
void setup() {
  Serial.begin(9600);
}

void loop() {
  int analogIn = analogRead(A0);
  float value = analogIn / 1023.0;
  Serial.println(value);
}
```

This code is written in the Arduino language. This language resembles the C, C++, and Java languages. It includes special constants, functions, and objects related to specific hardware capabilities of the Arduino board, such as analog inputs and serial ports.

This code consists of two functions, `setup()` and `loop()`. Both functions are required to be defined in any Arduino sketch. The `setup()` function is called once when the board is started (or restarted). After that, the `loop()` function is called repeatedly until the board is powered off, restarted, or reprogrammed.

The `setup()` function's body consists of one line that starts the connection via a built-in serial port of the board at a speed of `9600` bauds (that is, bits per second).

The `loop()` function's body consists of three lines. The first line reads the value from the board's analog input **A0**.

Each Arduino board has at least four analog input pins, which are referenced in the language as **A0**, **A1**, **A2**, and **A3** (see `arduino.cc/en/Products.Compare`). The `analogRead()` function reads a pin's voltage value and returns it as a 10-bit integer value (from 0 to 1023).

The second line divides this value by the maximal possible value `1023.0` to obtain a float value for `value` from `0` to `1`. The last line prints `value` with a new line character to the serial port.

A serial port is a way of transmitting data between the Arduino board and the computer. A little later, we will see how to read these printed values in the openFrameworks project.

The sketch is ready. Let's upload it to the board.

5. Connect the board to the computer using a USB cable.
6. Select your board type from the **Tools** | **Board** menu.
7. From the **Tools** | **Serial Port** menu, select the serial port of the computer to which Arduino is connected. (If there are several available ports in the menu, including USB and Bluetooth, choose USB.)

8. Compile and upload the sketch by clicking on the **Upload** button in the Arduino IDE (this button is denoted by a right arrow). When uploading is finished, you will see the **Done uploading** message at the bottom of the IDE window.

   Now our sketch is executing on the board. Let's check the values it outputs to the serial port.

9. Click on the **Serial Monitor** button located in the top-right corner of the IDE window. The **Serial Monitor** window will appear. This window shows data received via the serial port from the board. In our case, it will be numbers from `0` to `1`, as shown in the following screenshot:

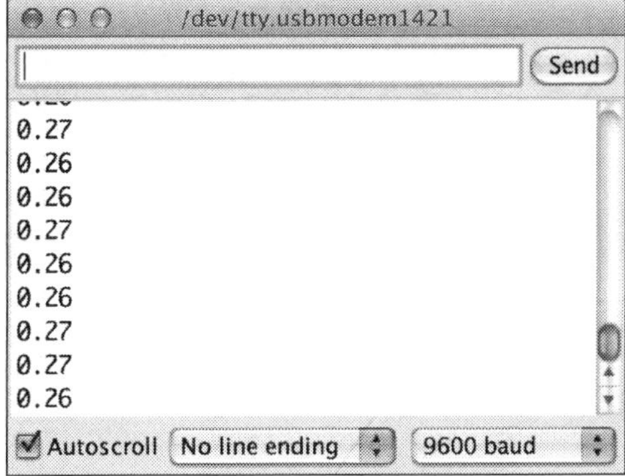

This is the Serial Monitor window of the Arduino IDE

> By default, the `Serial.println` output floats with two decimal places. If you need a better precision, you can specify exact number of decimal places as the second argument, for example:
>
> ```
> Serial.println(value, 4);
> ```
>
> The preceding line will output floats with four decimal places.

10. Now touch the **A0** pin of the board with your finger; the numbers will change because some voltage fluctuations will appear on this pin.

11. If you have a potentiometer, you can connect it to the Arduino board (normally, a potentiometer with an impedance of 10 kilo Ohm is used). First, unplug the board from the computer. Then, connect the potentiometer to **GND**, **A0**, and **5V** (or **3.3V**; it depends on your board's model) pins of the board, as shown in this image:

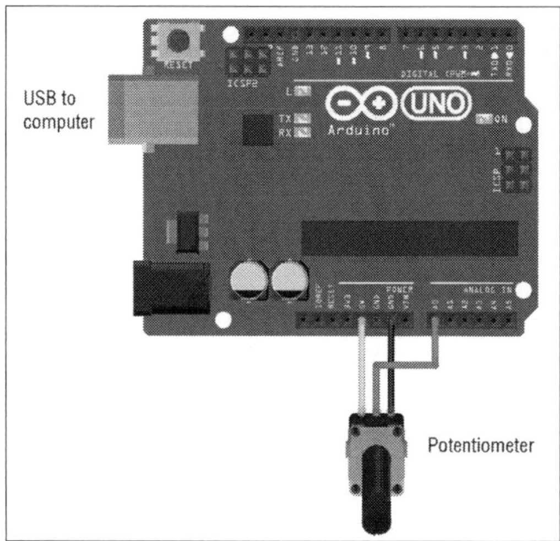

This shows the connecting of a potentiometer to an Arduino board

> This scheme was made with free open source software **Fritzing**, available at `fritzing.org`.

Now, by moving the potentiometer's wiper, you can precisely control Arduino's output numbers from `0` to `1`.

Our board is ready to be connected to the openFrameworks project. Let's do it.

Receiving data from Arduino in the openFrameworks project

To receive data from Arduino in openFrameworks, we can use the `ofSerial` class, which reads and writes data to a serial port. To implement it, perform the following steps:

1. Open the `VideoSynth` project if it is currently not open.
2. Add the following declarations to the `ofApp` class:

```
ofSerial serial;
string str;
```

The first line declares the `serial` object of the `ofSerial` class, and the second line declares the `str` string, which will be used as a buffer to collect the received text data.

3. Set up the serial port by adding the following code to `setup()`:

```
serial.setup( 0, 9600 );
```

It opens the first (index `0`) serial port in the list of available ports at a speed of `9600` bauds.

4. Add the code to receive and analyze data from Arduino to `update()`:

```
while ( true ) {
  int c = serial.readByte();
  if ( c == OF_SERIAL_NO_DATA || c == OF_SERIAL_ERROR || c == 0 )
    break;
  if ( c == '\n' ) {
    pinchY = ofToFloat( str );
    str = "";
  }
  else str.push_back( c );
}
```

The first line runs the infinite `while` loop. We will exit from this loop by calling `break` when we process all the data stored in the serial port's buffer at the moment.

The second line reads the next character from the serial port to the variable `c`.

Note that this variable has the type `int` (not `unsigned char`) to properly handle cases when `serial.readByte()` does not return a character but a negative value equal to the `OF_SERIAL_NO_DATA` or `OF_SERIAL_ERROR` constants.

The third line checks whether `c` is equal to `OF_SERIAL_NO_DATA`, `OF_SERIAL_ERROR`, or `0`. This means all data received by the serial port was already processed, some connection error occurred, or symbol with code `0` is received (the latter case occurs in Windows when Arduino is not connected). In this case, we exit from the loop by calling the `break` command.

The `if ( c == '\n' ) {` line checks whether a new line symbol (`\n`) was received. If so, we set a value to the `pinchY` slider stored in the `str` buffer. Also, we clear the buffer to be ready to receive the next value. In the opposite case, we append the received character to the buffer.

The openFrameworks project is ready to work with Arduino. Before running it, close the **Serial Monitor** window in the Arduino IDE, because the serial port cannot be used by two programs simultaneously.

Run the project and use your finger or potentiometer to adjust the **pinchY** slider. Congratulations—the simple physical computing with Arduino and openFrameworks works!

Connection troubleshooting

If the **pinchY** slider does not change by the Arduino values, it's because you probably chose the incorrect serial port index in the `serial.setup(0, 9600)` command.

To resolve the issue, let's print out the list of all the available serial ports by adding the following command to `setup()`:

```
serial.listDevices();
```

On running the project, you will see a list of devices in the project's console output, such as the following:

```
[notice ] ofSerial: [0] = tty.usbmodem1421
[notice ] ofSerial: [1] = cu.usbmodem1421
[notice ] ofSerial: [2] = cu.Bluetooth-Modem
[notice ] ofSerial: [3] = tty.Bluetooth-Modem
```

In Windows and Linux, the console window runs together with the project; in OS X, it is shown inside the Xcode interface.

Here, the numbers in brackets (`[0]` and others) denote port indices. Choose the proper index of your Arduino device (it should correspond to the port that was chosen in the **Tools** | **Serial Port** Arduino IDE's menu) and set it as a first argument to the `serial.setup(..., 9600)` command.

Connecting more devices

In the considered example, we receive just one value from Arduino. In real projects, we often need to use several input devices. So, let's consider how to send two values from Arduino to our openFrameworks project.

On Arduino's side, let's print both values on one line and separate them by the space character, as shown in the following code for Arduino's `loop()` function:

```
float value0 = analogRead(A0) / 1023.0;
float value1 = analogRead(A1) / 1023.0;
Serial.print(value0);
Serial.print(" ");
Serial.println(value1);
```

On openFrameworks' side, let's split the received string `str` using the `ofSplitString()` function and use the resulting array of strings list to set values to the two sliders, as shown here (this code should be inserted instead of the `pinchY = ofToFloat( str )` command):

```
vector<string> list = ofSplitString( str, " " );
if ( list.size() >= 2 ) {
  pinchY = ofToFloat( list[0] );
  extrude = ofToFloat( list[1] );
}
```

The first line splits the string `str` to its parts using space as a delimiter, the second line checks that we have at least two strings in the resulted array list, and the third and fourth lines convert strings of list to float values and set them to the `pinchY` and `extrude` sliders.

Summary

In this chapter, we learned how to create distributed projects using the OSC networking protocol. At first, we implemented receiving OSC in our openFrameworks project. Next, we created a simple OSC sender project with openFrameworks. Then, we considered how to create an OSC sender on mobile devices using TouchOSC and also how to build senders using the Python and Max/MSP languages. Now, we can control the video synthesizer from other computers or mobile devices via networking.

Finally, we considered a simple example of physical computing that uses Arduino with a connected potentiometer to control a slider in the openFrameworks project.

In this chapter, we finished our video synthesizer project. In the next chapter, we will consider how to run its lighter version on the iOS, Android, and Raspberry Pi devices.

8
Deploying the Project on iOS, Android, and Raspberry Pi

In the previous chapters, we developed an openFrameworks project for a desktop computer (OS X, Windows, or Linux). But, as you may know, openFrameworks is implemented on most popular mobile platforms, including iOS, Android, and Raspberry Pi devices. So in this chapter, we will dig into mobile development with openFrameworks; running our video synthesizer project on all these devices.

Mobile platforms have some specifics, so things such as shaders must be elaborated when porting from a desktop project to a mobile project. To have more fun, we will consider not the final, but a simpler version of our video synthesizer project. We will use the video synthesizer developed in *Chapter 3, Adding a GUI and Handling Keyboard Events*; it consists of Pattern Generator (matrix) and a GUI panel. This synthesizer is simple, yet still powerful enough to demonstrate basic capabilities of openFrameworks for mobiles.

We will have a look at the following topics:

- Installing software for developing with openFrameworks on iOS, Android, and Raspberry Pi devices
- Creating and running project on iOS, Android, and Raspberry Pi devices
- Using accelerometer on iOS and Android devices

Working with iOS, Android, and Raspberry Pi devices is described in separate sections independently, so you can jump to reading about the most interesting device immediately.

Running the project on an iOS device

In this section, we will create a video synthesizer project and run it on iOS Simulator and an iOS device. The project will be based on code we developed in *Chapter 3, Adding a GUI and Handling Keyboard Events*.

If you have no source code for the project we made in *Chapter 3, Adding a GUI and Handling Keyboard Events*, please get it from the example code files for this book.

To develop iOS projects, you must have a computer running OS X (such as MacBook, Mac Pro or Mac mini). This is mandatory before you go ahead with this section.

To deploy the project on a real iOS device and publish it on the Apple App Store, you need two things:

- An iOS device (iPhone, iPad, or iPod touch)
- An iOS Developer License from Apple (this costs $99 per year; you can buy it at `developer.apple.com/programs`)

You can still develop a project and run it in iOS Simulator without this license but can't upload it on your iOS device and publish on the App Store.

Let's prepare the required software:

1. Install Xcode (if you haven't installed it yet) from the Mac App Store. It's a free IDE for developing OS X and iOS applications using the C++, C, and Objective C programming languages.
2. Download openFrameworks for iOS from `openframeworks.cc/download` and unzip it.
3. Check whether Xcode and openFrameworks for iOS work together. Open any example project in Xcode contained in openFrameworks' unzipped `examples` folder, then build and run it; the example runs in iOS Simulator.

Now let's begin developing our own project for iOS by creating an empty project using Project Generator:

1. Run the Project Generator wizard (you should run it from the unzipped openFrameworks for iOS folder, but not from openFrameworks for OS X that we considered in previous chapters).
2. Set the project name as `VideoSynth`.

3. Add the `ofxGUI` addon to the project.
4. Click on the **GENERATE PROJECT** button.

[See details on working with Project Generator in the *Creating and running a new project* section of *Chapter 2, Creating Your First openFrameworks Project*.]

The project is created. Open it in Xcode and discover its structure. The project contains three source files: `main.mm`, `ofApp.h`, and `ofApp.mm`. They play the same role as `main.cpp`, `ofApp.h`, and `ofApp.cpp` considered in detail in the *Discovering the project's code structure* section in *Chapter 2, Creating Your First openFrameworks Project*. The only difference is in using the extension `mm` instead of `cpp`, which means it's an Objective-C/C++ module. So you can mix C++ and Objective-C (native for iOS) constructions in your code whenever it is needed.

The other difference is in the `ofApp` class. To see it, open the `ofApp.h` file. The class has the same structure as in a desktop openFrameworks project but has a different set of events. For example, `mouse...` functions are replaced with `touch...` functions. They respond to touching the device screen with a finger or fingers and provide you with plenty of information about touching, such as position, number of touches, size of the touching zone, and pressure.

Implementing video synthesizer for iOS

Let's fill our empty project with the code of the video synthesizer from *Chapter 3, Adding a GUI and Handling Keyboard Events*, (more precisely, we mean all the code we created in *Chapter 2, Creating Your First openFrameworks Project*, and *Chapter 3, Adding a GUI and Handling Keyboard Events*):

1. Include the `ofxGui` addon's header to the `ofApp.h` file by inserting the following line (after all other `#include ...` commands):

   ```
   #include "ofxGui.h"
   ```

2. Copy the declarations of the functions `stripePattern()` and `matrixPattern()`, and all the objects from the `ofApp` class we had in *Chapter 3, Adding a GUI and Handling Keyboard Events*, to the current `ofApp` class, as follows:

   ```
   void stripePattern();
   ofxPanel gui;
   ...
   void matrixPattern();
   ```

Do not copy the declaration of the `exit()` function because it is declared in the class already. In the opposite case, you will get a compiling error.

3. Copy the `setup()` function's body from the `ofApp.cpp` file we have in *Chapter 3, Adding a GUI and Handling Keyboard Events*, to the current `ofApp.mm` file, as follows:

   ```
   ofSetWindowTitle( "Video synth" );
   ofSetWindowShape( 1280, 720 );
   ...
   showGui = true;
   ```

   Comment out the `ofSetWindowTitle...` and `ofSetWindowShape...` commands because they are not needed here.

4. Replace `"settings.xml"` in the `gui.loadFromFile( "settings.xml" )` command in `setup()` with the `ofxiPhoneGetDocumentsDirectory() + "settings.xml"` expression.

   The `ofxiPhoneGetDocumentsDirectory()` function returns a path to the `Documents` directory of our application. This directory is managed by iOS, and it is the place where we can write and read our own files during the application's execution. So, after such modification, the `gui.loadFromFile...` command will read the `settings.xml` file from this directory.

See details on the `Documents` directory in the File System Programming Guide document available at `developer.apple.com/library`.

5. Copy the whole of the `stripePattern()` and `matrixPattern()` functions and the bodies of the `draw()` and `exit()` functions.
6. Again, replace `"settings.xml"` in `exit()` by `ofxiPhoneGetDocumentsDirectory() + "settings.xml"`.

   The project is almost ready. The only thing we don't implement is the reaction on the keyboard events implemented in the `keyPressed()` function of the original desktop project. Compared with desktops, using a keyboard on a mobile is a complex process: we need to show the keyboard, work with it, and finally hide it.

So, here we will not implement keyboard responding, but implement one action from our desktop project: toggling the visibility of the GUI panel. We will do it when the user double-taps the device's screen. Here's how we accomplish this:

7. Add the following code to the `touchDoubleTap()` function:

```
showGui = !showGui;
```

   This line toggles the visibility of the GUI by double-tapping.

Now, the project is ready. Click on the **Run** button in Xcode and the project will be built and run in iOS Simulator.

iOS Simulator is a separate application that is installed together with Xcode automatically. It lets you test the basic functionality of iOS applications on the desktop without uploading on a real device.

You will see the iOS Simulator window, which looks like an iPhone, with our project running in it, as shown in the following screenshot:

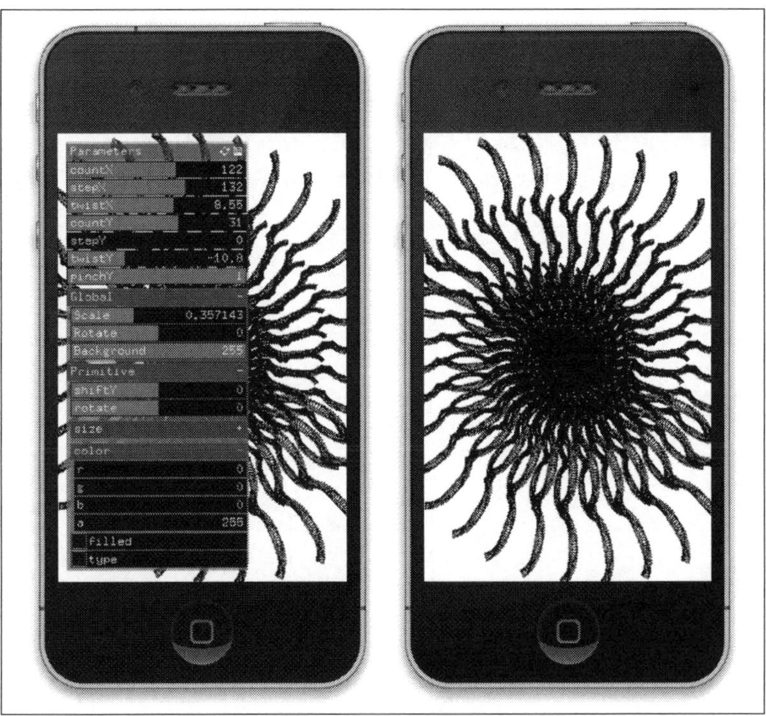

Here's the video synthesizer running in iOS Simulator

Use the mouse to adjust the sliders. Also, double-click on the project's screen to hide and show the GUI panel. Click on the **Home** button in iOS Simulator to close the project. This causes the `exit()` function to be called and saves the GUI state, so on the next project's run, this GUI state will be restored.

The `exit()` function is called when you click on the **Home** button in iOS Simulator, but it is not being called when you interrupt the execution by clicking on the **Stop** button in Xcode.

Building a project for iPad

By default, Xcode builds and runs project for iPhone. To build it and run in Simulator for iPad, do the following:

1. Click on **VideoSynth** in the left-hand side of the Xcode window to show the project settings in the central part of Xcode.
2. Select **TARGETS** as **VideoSynth** to see the settings for this target.

Target is an actual executable file of our project made by the compiler.

3. Switch from **iPhone** to **iPad** in the listbox in the **Deployment Info** tab there. Now our project is configured to build for iPad.

   These three steps are illustrated in the following screenshot:

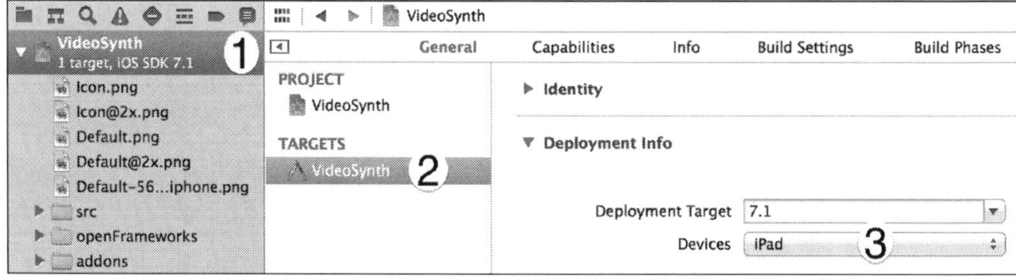

This shows how the project is configured to be compiled for iPad

4. Finally, choose an iPad device in iOS Simulator by clicking the listbox of the available devices, located in the top-left corner of the Xcode window, as shown in this screenshot:

This shows the selecting of an iPad device in iOS Simulator

5. Now, click on the **Run** button in Xcode. The project will be built for iPad and run in Simulator with the iPad device.

> You can change the size of iPad in the iOS Simulator window by navigating to its **Window** | **Scale** menu.

Deploying the project on an iOS device

If you have an iOS device, you can deploy our project on it. Before you can do that, you need to buy iOS Developer License from Apple (it costs $99 per year; see details at `developer.apple.com/programs`). Next, you should create a provisioning profile for the mobile device and a development certificate for your computer.

See the detailed instructions on this at `openframeworks.cc/setup/iphone`.

Using accelerometer

A typical iOS device has an **accelerometer** and a **gyroscope** to detect the motion and the orientation of the device respectively. openFrameworks has a built-in `ofxAccelerometer` class, which handles the accelerometer. Let's implement using it to control two sliders of the project using the following steps:

1. Add the initialization of the accelerometer to `setup()`:

```
ofxAccelerometer.setup();
```

2. Add the following commands to `update()` for getting the accelerometer's values and using them:

```
ofPoint ori = ofxAccelerometer.getOrientation();
twistX = ori.x;
twistY = ori.y;
```

The first line gets the current orientation angles of accelerometer. So, `ori.x`, `ori.y`, and `ori.z` are rotation angles around the *X*, *Y*, and *Z* axes of the device respectively. Angles are measured in degrees.

The second and third lines set orientation angles around the *X* and *Y* axes to the sliders `twistX` and `twistY` respectively.

[If you want to get a vector of the device's acceleration, use the `ofxAccelerometer.getForce()` method.]

Run the project on a device and tilt the device. You will see that the **twistX** slider values depend on the tilt across the device (because it is equal to tilt around the *X* axis), and the **twistY** slider values depend on the tilt along the device (because it is equal to the rotation around the *Y* axis).

[Using an accelerometer gives interesting results only on a real iOS device. iOS Simulator's accelerometer returns the fixed values and is not useful for this purpose.]

Congratulations, the simple video synthesizer working on iOS and using the accelerometer is ready!

Running the project on an Android device

In this section, we will create a video synthesizer project and run it on an Android device. The project will be based on the code we developed in *Chapter 3, Adding a GUI and Handling Keyboard Events*.

[If you have no source codes for the project we made in *Chapter 3, Adding a GUI and Handling Keyboard Events*, please get it from the example code files for this book.]

To develop Android projects, you need a computer (OS X, Linux, or Windows) and the Android device itself.

Apps for Android OS are primarily written using Java-oriented **Android SDK** (**Android Software Development Kit**). For developing using the C++ language (and hence for developing with openFrameworks), we need to use **Android NDK** (**Android Native Development Kit**). Currently NDK is not as mature as SDK is.

So, for developing openFrameworks projects for Android, you need to set up a special IDE supporting both SDK and NDK. Currently, openFrameworks works with the Eclipse IDE.

The official IDE for Android development is the Android Studio IDE, and it is expected that new releases of openFrameworks will work with it.

Installing software for Android development

To install the required software for developing (SDK, NDK, IDE, and openFrameworks), follow the instructions at `openframeworks.cc/setup/android-eclipse`.

Currently (April 2015), these instructions are a little out of a date, so please consider the following clarifications about the installation process:

- The instructions at `openframeworks.cc/setup/android-eclipse` describe how to install and configure the **Android Development Tools** (**ADT**) bundle, which is the Eclipse IDE together with ADT and SDK. Currently the ADT bundle is out of development, so you need to download and install Eclipse, the ADT plugin, and SDK separately. If you have difficulties with such installing, you can still download and use the ADT bundle at `stackoverflow.com/questions/27449206/what-is-the-final-version-of-the-adt-bundle`.
- Install the NDK version r9b or later.
- When setting up the `NDK_ROOT` and `SDK_ROOT` paths in the `paths.make` file, avoid using the ~ (home directory) symbol; for example, use a path such as `/Users/perevalovds/Android/android-ndk-r9b` instead of `~/Android/android-ndk-r9b` (this recommendation is for OS X and Linux only).
- After the first start of Eclipse, disable the automatic building of all projects by unchecking the **Project** | **Build Automatically** menu item.
- When importing openFrameworks examples from `openFrameworks/examples/android` to Eclipse, it is a good idea to uncheck all projects in the list except `androidEmptyExample`. Later, you can import other examples when they are needed.
- When enabling the debugging mode on an Android device, note that *Developer options* can be hidden by default. See `developer.android.com/tools/device.html` about enabling it.

After installing, deploy the `androidEmptyExample` example on your Android device to check that all is installed properly.

Implementing video synthesizer for Android

Now let's create a video synthesizer project. Currently, there is no Project Generator for the Android version of openFrameworks. So, we will create the project by copying the existing example, namely `androidGuiExample` (because we need the `ofxGui` addon).

Creating an empty project

Perform the following steps to create a new, clean project:

1. Copy the `androidGuiExample` folder to a new folder named `VideoSynth` (place it in the same folder, `examples/android`).
2. Open Eclipse and open the project by clicking on the **File | Import...** menu, selecting the **General | Existing Projects into Workspace** type, choosing the `examples/android` folder, and checking only our `VideoSynth` folder there. (The steps are the same as when we import the example `androidEmptyExample` mentioned earlier).
3. Clear the `ofApp` class in `ofApp.h` from all the members, except the `setup()`, `update()`, and `draw()` functions.
4. Delete all the function definitions in `ofApp` except the `setup()`, `update()`, and `draw()` functions. Then, clear their bodies' code.

Now we have an empty project with the `ofxGui` addon linked to it.

Implementing the video synthesizer

Let's fill our empty project with the code of the video synthesizer from *Chapter 3, Adding a GUI and Handling Keyboard Events*, (more precisely, we mean all the code we create in *Chapter 2, Creating Your First openFrameworks Project*, and *Chapter 3, Adding a GUI and Handling Keyboard Events*) by performing the following steps:

1. Copy the declarations of the `stripePattern()` and `matrixPattern()` functions and all the objects from the `ofApp` class we have in *Chapter 3, Adding a GUI and Handling Keyboard Events*, to the current `ofApp` class:

   ```
   void stripePattern();
   ofxPanel gui;
   ...
   void matrixPattern();
   ```

> Do not copy the declaration of the `exit()` function because it is not needed here.

2. Copy the `setup()` function's body from the `ofApp.cpp` file we had in *Chapter 3, Adding a GUI and Handling Keyboard Events,* to the current `ofApp.cpp` file:

   ```
   ofSetWindowTitle( "Video synth" );
   ofSetWindowShape( 1280, 720 );
   ...
   showGui = true;
   ```

   Comment out the `ofSetWindowTitle...` and `ofSetWindowShape...` commands because they are not needed here.

3. Copy the whole of the `stripePattern()` and `matrixPattern()` functions and the body of the `draw()` function.

The project is almost ready. The things we haven't implemented yet are saving the GUI state (this was implemented in `exit()`) and the reaction on keyboard events (this was implemented in `keyPressed()`). We will discuss these and also implement the accelerometer's usage a little bit later. Now it's time to run the project!

Build the project and run it on your device. You will see the working video synthesizer with a GUI panel, as shown in the following screenshot:

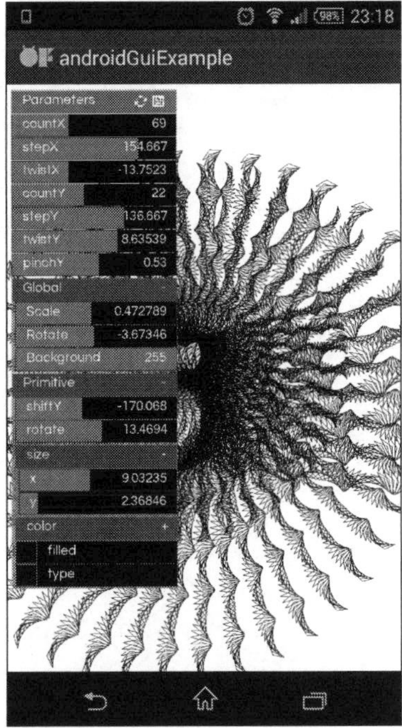

This shows the video synthesizer running on an Android device

Increasing the size of the GUI panel

If you see that the GUI panel on the device's screen looks too small, add the following code to the beginning of the `setup()` function:

```
ofxGuiSetFont("Questrial-Regular.ttf",18,true,true);
ofxGuiSetTextPadding(20);
ofxGuiSetDefaultWidth(300);
ofxGuiSetDefaultHeight(40);
```

This code is taken from the original `androidGuiExample` project, which we used as the starting point for our Android project. The first line loads the font used by the GUI from the `Questrial-Regular.ttf` file. The second argument, `18`, specifies the font size. The remaining lines of the code specify new dimensional parameters of a GUI panel.

Run the project and you will see that the GUI panel is now bigger.

Troubleshooting

If, while developing, your project suddenly stops building and Eclipse reports compiling errors, use the following hints to resolve the issue and start to build the project again:

- Wait while Eclipse starts entirely before starting the building process. Eclipse loads and updates Android SDK, which can take from several seconds to a minute. See the **Progress** tab in the bottom-right corner of the IDE window for details on the loading process.
- Stop the app on the device before compiling.
- Clear the contents of the `bin` folder of your project (but keep the `data` subfolder untouched if it exists).
- Restart Eclipse.
- Clean the project by clicking on the **Project** | **Clean...** menu.
- If a compiler error related to the `AndroidManifest.xml` file occurs, open this file for editing and change it a little (for example, insert a new line at the end of the file) and save the file.

Now, let's implement saving the GUI state and implement hiding the GUI by double-tapping.

Implementing reaction on stopping and double-tapping

In openFrameworks for Android, the `exit()` function is not called when the project stops executing. Instead of this function, we need to use the `pause()` and `stop()` functions.

Considering the keyboard events, which we did in the desktop version of our project but omitted in Android version, let's note that using a keyboard on a mobile is quite a complex process. We need to show the keyboard, work with it, and finally hide it. So, here we will not implement keyboard responding, but implement one action from our desktop project: toggling the visibility of the GUI panel. We will do this when the user double-taps the device's screen.

To implement the reaction on stopping and double-tapping, we need to change the base class name of the `ofApp` class from `ofBaseApp` to `ofxAndroidApp` and add the new functions `touchDoubleTap()`, `pause()`, and `stop()` to the `ofApp` class.

> See the `androidTouchExample` example for a list of all available Android-related functions, such as `touchDown()`, `resume()`, and `backPressed()`.

Let's do this by performing the following steps:

1. Add the `ofxAndroid` header to `ofApp.h`, as follows:

   ```
   #include "ofxAndroid.h"
   ```

2. Change the base class name of the `ofApp` class from `ofBaseApp` to `ofxAndroidApp`. To achieve this, replace the `class ofApp : public ofBaseApp{` line with the following line:

   ```
   class ofApp : public ofxAndroidApp{
   ```

3. Add the declaration of new functions to the `ofApp` class:

   ```
   void touchDoubleTap(int x, int y, int id);
   void pause();
   void stop();
   ```

4. Add the definition of the `touchDoubleTap()` function to the `ofApp.cpp` file:

   ```
   void ofApp::touchDoubleTap(int x, int y, int id) {
     showGui = !showGui;
   }
   ```

   This function toggles the visibility of the GUI when the user double-taps the screen.

5. Add the definitions of the `pause()` and `stop()` functions to the `ofApp.cpp` file:

   ```
   void ofApp::pause() {
     gui.saveToFile( "settings.xml" );
   }
   void ofApp::stop() {
     gui.saveToFile( "settings.xml" );
   }
   ```

   These functions save the state of the GUI to the `"settings.xml"` file right before the project is paused or stopped.

Run the project and double-tap the screen to toggle the GUI panel's visibility. Also, if you stop the project and start it again, the GUI state will be restored.

The last thing we will consider in our Android project is using the accelerometer.

Using the accelerometer on an Android device

A typical Android device has an **accelerometer** and a **gyroscope** for detecting the motion and the orientation, respectively, of the device. openFrameworks has a built-in `ofxAccelerometer` class, which handles the accelerometer. Let's implement using it to control two sliders of the project by performing the following steps:

1. Add the `ofxAccelerometer` header to `ofApp.h`, as follows:

   ```
   #include "ofxAccelerometer.h"
   ```

2. Add the initialization of the accelerometer to `setup()`:

   ```
   ofxAccelerometer.setup();
   ```

3. Add the following commands to `update()` for getting the accelerometer's values and using them:

   ```
   ofPoint ori = ofxAccelerometer.getOrientation();
   twistX = ori.x;
   twistY = ori.y;
   ```

   The first line gets the current orientation angles of the accelerometer. So, `ori.x`, `ori.y` and `ori.z` are rotation angles around the *X*, *Y*, and *Z* axes of device respectively. Angles are measured in degrees.

   The second and third lines set the orientation angles around the *X* and *Y* axes to the sliders `twistX` and `twistY` respectively.

If you want to get a vector of the device's acceleration, use the `ofxAccelerometer.getForce()` method.

Run the project on your device and tilt the device. You will see that the **twistX** slider values depend on the tilt across the device (because it is equal to tilting around the *X* axis), and the **twistY** slider values depends on the tilt along the device (because it is equal to rotation around the *Y* axis).

Congratulations, the simple video synthesizer working on Android and using accelerometer is ready!

Renaming the project

Currently our project is named **androidGuiExample**. If you want to rename it, see the instructions in the **Creating new applications** section available at `openframeworks.cc/setup/android-eclipse`.

Running the project on Raspberry Pi

In this section, we will create a video synthesizer project and run it on a Raspberry Pi device. The project will be based on the code we developed in *Chapter 3, Adding a GUI and Handling Keyboard Events.*

> If you have no source code for the project we made in *Chapter 3, Adding a GUI and Handling Keyboard Events*, please get it from the example code files for this book.

Note that as Raspberry Pi does not work very fast, the complete process of its setup from installing the OS to building and running the video synthesizer project can take up to three hours (for the first generation of Raspberry Pi devices).

> To speed up the compilation, you might use the **cross compiling** technique, which involves compiling on another (more powerful) computer. See the details on this at `www.openframeworks.cc/setup/raspberrypi/Raspberry-Pi-Cross-compiling-guide.html`.

Required equipment

To proceed with this section, you need the following equipment:

- A Raspberry Pi device (refer to `www.raspberrypi.org/products`)
- An SD card with a capacity of at least 4 GB with Raspbian OS or **New Out of Box Software** (**NOOBS**) installed

Raspbian OS is an operating system on which we will install openFrameworks. NOOBS is a collection of several operating systems ready to be installed on the first run of the device (refer to `www.raspberrypi.org/introducing-noobs`).

- To prepare such an SD, follow the instructions at `www.raspberrypi.org/downloads` or buy a ready-to-use SD card with NOOBS preinstalled
- A computer monitor or TV panel with HDMI or DVI input
- A USB mouse and a keyboard
- A microUSB-USB cable to power Raspberry Pi
- A cable HDMI-HDMI or HDMI-DVI to connect Raspberry Pi to a monitor or TV panel
- A networking cable to connect Raspberry Pi to your networking router

Setting up the device

Let's start the Raspberry Pi device by performing the following steps:

1. Insert the SD card into the Raspberry Pi.
2. Connect the Raspberry Pi to the monitor, mouse, keyboard, and networking router.
3. Power on the monitor.
4. Connect the Raspberry Pi to the USB-source of power using microUSB-USB cable (such a source can be the USB port of a laptop or power adapter for a mobile phone with USB output).

   The device will be started.
5. Follow the instructions that appear to set up Raspbian Pi.

   Use the cursor keys and *Tab* to navigate in the configurer program.

   You should finish setting up the graphical desktop screen, which resembles Windows / Linux desktops.

   If you see the text line input instead of the graphical desktop, type `startx` to run it, or the `Raspi-config` command to run the configurer again.

Now we are ready to install openFrameworks.

Installing openFrameworks

Here, we will basically follow the instructions at `openframeworks.cc/setup/raspberrypi/Raspberry-Pi-Getting-Started.html`. Perform the following steps to accomplish this:

1. Run the *LXTerminal* application by double-clicking on its icon. The terminal window appears, as shown in the following screenshot:

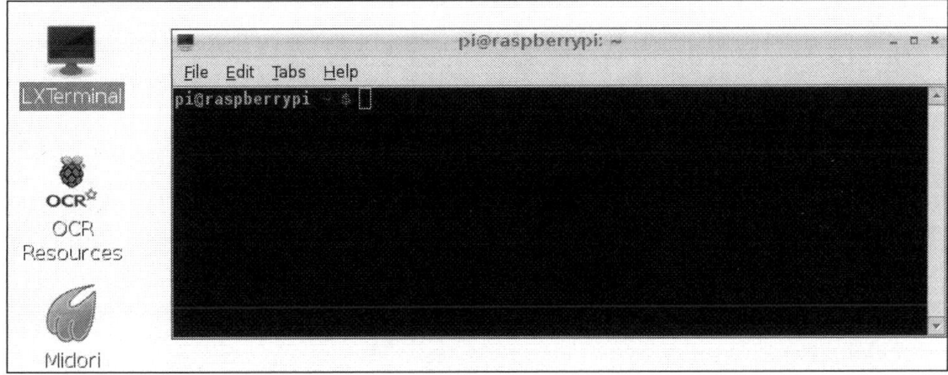

This is the terminal window in the graphical desktop of Raspberry Pi

2. Download openFrameworks by typing the following command in LXTerminal:

```
curl -O http://www.openframeworks.cc/versions/v0.8.4/of_v0.8.4_
linuxarmv6l_release.tar.gz
```

   Note that this is one long command; you should type it in one line.

3. Create the `openFrameworks` folder as follows:

```
mkdir openFrameworks
```

4. Unpack the downloaded archive as follows:

```
tar vxfz of_v0.8.4_linuxarmv6l_release.tar.gz -C openFrameworks
--strip-components 1
```

You need not type long filenames completely. Just begin typing and press *Tab*. The terminal will complete the filename or the folder name.

5. Now let's install dependencies, that is, libraries needed for openFrameworks, by using the following commands:

```
cd openFrameworks/scripts/linux/debian_armv6l
sudo ./install_dependencies.sh
```

The last symbol in `debian_armv6l` is lowercase *L*.

The first command changes the current directory to `.../debian_armv6l`, and the second line starts installing dependencies. This process can take a while, up to half an hour. During installation, you will be asked to press *Y* (yes) or *N* (no); in all cases, press *Y*.

6. We are ready to perform the final step—build openFrameworks. Do it by using the following commands:

```
cd ~
cd openFrameworks/libs/openFrameworksCompiled/project
make Release -C
```

The first command sets the returned directory to home directory. The second command changes the current directory to the place where we should perform building. The last command starts building openFrameworks. Note that it can take about an hour to complete (depending on your Raspberry Pi model).

Running the first example

Let's build and run the `guiExample` example by performing the following steps:

1. Go to the home directory by using the following command:

```
cd ~
```

2. Go to the example's folder by using the following command:

```
cd openFrameworks/examples/gui/guiExample
```

3. Build the example by using the following command:

```
make
```

The building process can take about 10 minutes.

4. Run the example by using the following command:

```
./bin/guiExample
```

5. Press *Esc* to close the application.

You can build and run any other example in a similar way. To discover which examples exist in openFrameworks, you can use the `ls` command in the terminal to list a folder's contents. Another way is using the **File Manager** application, which you can run by clicking in the bottom-left corner of the desktop to show a list of all programs, and selecting **Assessories | File Manager**.

Implementing a video synthesizer for Raspberry Pi

Now, let's create the video synthesizer project. Currently, there is no Project Generator for the Raspberry Pi version of openFrameworks. Hence, we will create our project from the existing example, namely `guiExample` considered earlier (because we need the `ofxGui` addon), using the following steps:

1. Copy the `guiExample` folder to the `openFrameworks/apps/myApps` folder and rename it to `VideoSynth`. The simplest way to do this is using **File Manager**.
2. Copy the `ofApp.h` and `ofApp.cpp` files made in *Chapter 3, Adding a GUI and Handling Keyboard Events*, to the `VideoSynth/src` folder (by rewriting existing files).
3. Go to the project's folder:

   ```
   cd ~
   cd openFrameworks/apps/myApps/VideoSynth
   ```

4. As we replace the source files, it is desirable to clean the project before building using the following command:

   ```
   make clean
   ```

   You should do cleaning only after substantial changes of source code or after replacing the source files.

5. Build the project using this command:

   ```
   make
   ```

6. Run the project using this command:

   ```
   ./bin/VideoSynth
   ```

Notice that our video synthesizer looks and works exactly like its desktop version. Congratulations! We successfully ported the simple video synthesizer to Raspberry Pi!

> To shut down Raspberry Pi, use the following command:
> `sudo poweroff`

Summary

In this chapter, we considered developing projects on iOS, Android, and Raspberry Pi. We covered installing the software necessary for developing, running an example, and implementing a simple video synthesizer. Also, we showed how to use the accelerometer in iOS and Android devices.

This is the last chapter devoted to learning openFrameworks. In the next and final chapter, we will discuss the directions to further study openFrameworks and enhance the video synthesizer.

9
Further Resources

Until now, we have investigated the basics of openFrameworks and created the video synthesizer project.

In this last chapter, we will point out the resources and topics that may be helpful for your further exploration of openFrameworks and creative coding by covering the following topics:

- Enhancing the video synthesizer project
- Getting more information on openFrameworks
- Debugging and speeding up your code

> During the chapter, we will mention some classes and functions without detailed explanation. You can find information about them in the openFrameworks documentation at `openframeworks.cc/documentation` and in the openFrameworks' examples (which are placed in the `examples` folder).

Enhancing the video synthesizer project

Now, we will consider various ways of enhancing our video synthesizer and expanding its capabilities. If you don't want to improve it right now, feel free to skip this section and go to the next section that discusses books and other references to openFrameworks.

Speeding up the rendering

In *Chapter 2, Creating Your First openFrameworks Project*, and *Chapter 3, Adding a GUI and Handling Keyboard Events*, we considered drawing patterns made from geometric primitives. You would note that when the number of drawn primitives is high, the rendering frame rate becomes low. This is due to the fact that each primitive is drawn by sending a separate command to a video card.

To speed up the rendering, you need to rewrite the `stripePattern` and `matrixPattern` functions so that they use `ofMesh` objects or `ofVboMesh` classes to render primitives (instead of calling the `ofRect()` and `ofTriangle()` functions). These classes draw primitives in bulk using *one* command, and as a result, they work faster.

> Another option is using the `glDraw()` function of the OpenGL library. This library is used by openFrameworks to render anything. See the details on the usage of this function in the OpenGL library reference.

Drawing curves and text

In *Chapter 2, Creating Your First openFrameworks Project*, we considered drawing only lines, triangles, rectangles, and circles. To extend expression capabilities of the project, you can draw arbitrary filled figures and Bezier curves using the `ofPolyline` or `ofPath` classes. Also, you can output strings of text using the `ofDrawBitmapString` function or the `ofTrueTypeFont` class.

For example, to draw the current frame rate of the application on the screen, add the following command to the `ofApp::draw()` function:

```
ofDrawBitmapString( ofToString( ofGetFrameRate() ), 250, 20 );
```

The `ofGetFrameRate` function returns the frame rate as a float number, `ofToString` converts it into a string, and `ofDrawBitMapString` draws it at the position (`250`, `20`) on the screen.

Using fragment shaders for image generation

In *Chapter 4, Working with Raster Graphics – Images, Videos, and Shaders*, we considered using fragment shaders for image transformation. However, you can use fragment shaders to generate completely new images!

Furthermore, you can develop a shader online using a site such as `shadertoy.com`, and then port the shader to your openFrameworks project.

As an example, see how we ported the beautiful shader *Apollonian Fractures* by Otavio Good at `www.shadertoy.com/view/XdjSzD` to the openFrameworks project (with small modifications): `github.com/kuflex/examples/tree/master/ApollFrac`. The project generates animated pictures such as this:

This is a screenshot generated by Otavio Good's fragment shader ported from shadertoy.com to the openFrameworks project

Using vertex shaders for an object deformation

At the end of *Chapter 5, Creating 3D Graphics*, we deformed the 3D sphere vertex per vertex in C++ code. This approach works fast enough only when the number of vertices is small. To deform 3D (or 2D) objects containing millions of vertices, use a vertex shader; it processes vertices on a video card right before drawing it on the screen, and it works extremely fast.

See `gl/shaderExample` for details on using a vertex shader to deform objects.

Using the Firmata protocol for Arduino connection

In *Chapter 7, Distributed and Physical Computing with Networking and Arduino*, we considered the simplest case of reading data from one analog input of an Arduino device. It was really simple to implement. But for more complex tasks, such as getting several inputs and sending output signals to devices connected to Arduino (such as servos), more complex programming is required.

To simplify the input and output data from Arduino to computer, there is a standard protocol called **Firmata**. To discover it, see openFrameworks' `communication/firmataExample` example.

Multidisplay setup and sharing images between separate programs

The picture generated by our video synthesizer can be output directly to the screen or projector. As we considered in *Chapter 2, Creating Your First openFrameworks Project*, you can set an application to the fullscreen mode using the `ofSetFullScreen(true)` command or the `ofToggleFullScreen()` command.

For live performances, one screen could be insufficient. If you need to use a multidisplay setup, consider using the `ofAppGLFWWindow` class; see `forum.openframeworks.cc/t/of-0-8-multiple-screens/13059`.

Also, it is possible to send images between programs working on the same or separate computers using TCP networking implemented in the classes `ofxTCPServer` and `ofxTCPClient`. To obtain better results, it is preferable to use 1 GB networking or faster.

In our book *Mastering openFrameworks: Creative Coding Demystified, Packt Publishing*, we discuss an example of such image streaming using TCP networking.

Finally (currently on OS X only), an application's screen picture can be easily incorporated into a more complex video engine. For example, it can be passed to the *VDMX5* or to the *MadMapper* programs. Such a transmission of images between separate programs (running on the same computer) is possible with the **Syphon** protocol. It is implemented in the `ofxSyphon` addon. You can download it from `www.ofxaddons.com`.

We have discussed some straightforward improvements that you can implement in a video synthesizer for its *serious* use. Now, we will consider books and other references to openFrameworks that help to discover capabilities of openFrameworks not covered in this book.

Getting more information on openFrameworks

Our book was dedicated to the basics of openFrameworks with the main effort to create 2D and 3D generative graphics. So, we did not consider several topics such as computer vision and low-level sound synthesis. To get acquainted with the whole range of openFrameworks capabilities, check out the examples in the `examples` folder and explore the online documentation and forum at `openframeworks.cc`.

For a deeper understanding of openFrameworks, we recommend that you read other books on this subject.

openFrameworks books

Currently there are three books that cover openFrameworks:

- **ofBook**: This is a free online book on openFrameworks written collaboratively. It contains detailed information on many topics related to openFrameworks, C++ programming, and creative coding. To read it, go to the book's page at `github.com/openframeworks/ofBook`, click on the `chapters` folder, and you will see the list of chapters. Now click on the folder of the desired chapter, and click on the `chapter.md` file to read it.
- **Mastering openFrameworks: Creative Coding Demystified, Denis Perevalov, Packt Publishing, 2013**: This is our *big* book on openFrameworks, dedicated to low-level graphics, sound, and computer vision programming with openFrameworks.
- **Programming Interactivity: A Designer's Guide to Processing, Arduino, and openFrameworks, 2nd Edition, Joshua Noble, O'Reilly Media, 2012**: This is an extensive book about Processing, Arduino, and openFrameworks, covering many topics of interactive art, design, and the basics of programming for beginners.

Additionally, there are plenty of online lections and presentations covering various parts of openFrameworks, C++, and OpenGL.

Debugging and speeding up your code

We hope you went through the book easily. Now, when the video synthesizer is finished, we encourage you to imagine and implement your own project!

If you wish to make a project but have no idea what to do, explore projects at `www.creativeapplications.net` as a source of inspiration.

Now we'll give you some advice on debugging and optimizing your project's performance.

Debugging

The main rule for writing programs with fewer bugs is compiling and testing your project as often as possible.

If you detect incorrect behavior of the program, this probably means that some bug exists in the code. The main way to fix the bug is to locate it in the code. To achieve this, you can use the IDE's debugging tools, such as **breakpoints** and **watch list**.

You need to compile you project in the *debug* mode to be able to use the IDE's debugging tools.

Unfortunately, some errors in openFrameworks projects can be difficult to find if your project runs in the *debug* mode, because the project works too slowly and errors just don't occur. In this case, instead of the IDE's debugging, use printing diagnostic messages using the `cout` command (that means console output). For example, before starting the camera to grab, you can insert the following command:

```
cout << "Camera is starting" << endl;
```

Here `<<` is an **insertion operator** that sends symbols to the console; `endl` means **end of line** and generates a line break.

When this code executes, the message **Camera is starting** appears in the console window of your application.

openFrameworks has a special class `ofLog` for diagnostic messages. It allows the use of several levels of diagnostic messages and often is more handy than `cout`.

The other issue in the project is performance. Although openFrameworks is C++ based and provides fast implementation of your code on the CPU, the code must be written and compiled properly to be able to work fast; let's talk about it.

Speeding up the code

If you note that your project executes too slowly, check these optimization tips to improve the performance of the C++ code:

- Printing a diagnostic message takes time. So don't print them very often (especially in `for` and `while` cycles) because they, by themselves, can have a negative impact on performance. Also, remove (or comment out) messages that are not needed anymore.
- If the compiler is currently set to the *debug* scheme of compilation, switch it to the *release* mode. (In the *debug* mode, C++ code executes up to five times slower than in the *release* mode.)
- Before performing any optimization of bottlenecks in the code, make sure you detect them properly. To find bottlenecks, you can compute the time elapsed by a portion of the code by inserting the following lines before and after it:

  ```
  float time0 = ofGetElapsedTime();
  //... some code here
  cout << "time: " << ofGetElapsedTime() - time0 << endl;
  ```

  The first line stores the current time. The last line outputs a diagnostic message about the difference between the current and stored time in seconds.

Also, to detect bottlenecks in the code, you can use a special tool called **profiler**. It measures the execution time of each function in your project. Some IDEs contain a built-in profiler, but for some other IDEs, you should install it manually.

- When declaring functions, declare their parameters as references whenever it is possible. This is a powerful optimization technique that is often used in C++ codes. For example, consider a function getting a string as an input parameter:

  ```
  void myFunction( string s ) {
    //some code here…
  }
  ```

  If the `myFunction` function doesn't change `s`, you can declare this parameter as a constant reference:

  ```
  void myFunction( const string &s ) {
    //some code here...
  }
  ```

In the first case, each calling of `myFunction` leads to copying of the passed input string to a stack. Such a copy can take significant time in the case of large strings. In the second case, only the address of the string is passed. This operation takes almost no time, and the time taken does not depend on the string size.

- If, after some simple optimizations, your project still works slowly, you should consider using special tools, such as multithreading or GPU computing, which we will consider now:
    - If your computer has several cores, you can parallel your code's execution by multithread computations. Use the `ofThread` class to accomplish this.
    - If your computer has a powerful video card, you can put some computations to it, that is, use GPU technologies such as **fragment shaders**, **OpenCL**, or **compute shaders**. In openFrameworks, there is a great addon `ofxMSAOpenCL`, that allows you to utilize OpenCL technology for computing. You can download it from `www.ofxaddons.com`.

Summary

In this last chapter, we considered ways of improving the video synthesizer project and gave you some references to further study openFrameworks. Finally, we discussed tips on debugging and speeding up the code with openFrameworks.

To summarize what you have learned during the book, we prepared two appendices—*Appendix A, Video Synthesizer Reference*, is detailed video synthesizer documentation, and *Appendix B, openFrameworks Quick Reference*, contains a short reference to openFrameworks.

We wish you luck in developing your own outstanding projects and we hope openFrameworks will help you with it!

A

Video Synthesizer Reference

We developed quite an elaborated video synthesizer project through the entire book. To help you keep control over it, we've placed detailed references about all synthesizer parts in this appendix, including source files, data files, control keys, and GUI controls.

For convenience, the desktop and mobile versions are described separately.

The desktop version

The video synthesizer for desktop is the most elaborate in the book. It is discussed in the chapters from *Chapter 2, Creating Your First openFrameworks Project*, to *Chapter 7, Distributed and Physical Computing with Networking and Arduino*. It has a matrix pattern generator, shader-effect kaleidoscope, 3D rendering, GUI panel, and parameter automation, and can be controlled by the networking and Arduino devices.

The openFrameworks project and source files

The following is the project's code structure:

- The project uses the `ofxGui` (used in *Chapter 3, Adding a GUI and Handling Keyboard Events*) and `ofxOsc` (used in *Chapter 7, Distributed and Physical Computing with Networking and Arduino*) addons. They are linked to the project in the first stage of its creation using the Pattern Generator wizard in *Chapter 2, Creating Your First openFrameworks Project*.
- The project's source files are `ofApp.h` and `ofApp.cpp`. They are created and modified in *Chapter 2, Creating Your First openFrameworks Project*, and further extended in all chapters from *Chapter 3, Adding a GUI and Handling Keyboard Events*, to *Chapter 7, Distributed and Physical Computing with Networking and Arduino*. These source files are placed in the `src` folder of the project.

- The shader's code files, `kaleido.frag` and `kaleido.vert`, are created in *Chapter 4, Working with Raster Graphics – Images, Videos, and Shaders*. They are placed in the `bin/data` folder of the project.

Data files

The project works with the following data files stored in the `bin/data` folder:

- `settings.xml`: This file stores the GUI state. It saves and loads automatically. It is implemented in *Chapter 3, Adding a GUI and Handling Keyboard Events*.
- `collage.png`: This is an image file, loaded and drawn in *Chapter 4, Working with Raster Graphics – Images, Videos, and Shaders*.
- `flowing.mp4`: This is a video file, loaded and drawn in *Chapter 4, Working with Raster Graphics – Images, Videos, and Shaders*.
- `skvo.wav`: This is a music track, loaded and played in *Chapter 6, Animating Parameters*.
- `eeg.txt`: This is a text file with neural data, loaded and parsed in *Chapter 6, Animating Parameters*.

Also, the project saves screenshots to the `screen.png` file by pressing *Return* (*Enter*) and saves/loads the GUI presets by pressing *S* and *L*. It is implemented in *Chapter 3, Adding a GUI and Handling Keyboard Events*.

Control keys

The keys for controlling the project are the following:

Key	Action	Reference
Esc	This closes the application. It's a built-in feature of any openFrameworks application.	-
Z	This toggles the visibility of the GUI panel. This also toggles the mouse input for 3D camera navigating.	*Chapter 3, Adding a GUI and Handling Keyboard Events*, and *Chapter 5, Creating 3D Graphics*
Return (*Enter*)	This saves a screenshot to the `screenshot.png` file placed in the `bin/data` folder.	*Chapter 3, Adding a GUI and Handling Keyboard Events*
S	This saves the GUI state to an XML file. The file is chosen by dialog.	*Chapter 3, Adding a GUI and Handling Keyboard Events*
L	This loads the GUI state from an XML file. The file is chosen by dialog.	*Chapter 3, Adding a GUI and Handling Keyboard Events*

Key	Action	Reference
C	This starts the camera to grab video frames.	*Chapter 4, Working with Raster Graphics – Images, Videos, and Shaders*
P	This plays/stops the music track `skvo.wav` placed in the `bin/data` folder.	*Chapter 6, Animating Parameters*

The GUI controls

A GUI consists of one GUI panel, which includes a number of sliders and checkboxes. For convenience, some controls are combined in GUI groups (**Global**, **Primitive**, and **Mixer**). They are described in separate subsections. Note the following conventions:

- Notation *0..100* means that a slider takes integer values from 0 to 100
- Notation *[0, 100]* means that a slider takes float values in from 0 to 100
- All distances are measured in pixels. All angles are measured in degrees.

Basic sliders

These sliders control the geometry of the matrix pattern:

Name	Range	Description	Reference
countX	0..200	This controls the number of geometric primitives in the stripe pattern.	*Chapter 3, Adding a GUI and Handling Keyboard Events*
stepX	[0, 200]	This controls the distance between geometric primitives along the *X* axis in the stripe pattern.	*Chapter 3, Adding a GUI and Handling Keyboard Events*
twistX	[-45, 45]	This controls the rotation of each geometric primitive depending on its index in the stripe pattern. In *Chapter 6, Animating Parameters*, the slider's value is automated using data from the `eeg.txt` text file containing neural data recording.	*Chapter 3, Adding a GUI and Handling Keyboard Events*, and *Chapter 6, Animating Parameters*
countY	0..50	This controls the number of stripe patterns in the matrix pattern.	*Chapter 3, Adding a GUI and Handling Keyboard Events*
stepY	[0, 200]	This controls the distance between stripe patterns along the *Y* axis in the matrix pattern.	*Chapter 3, Adding a GUI and Handling Keyboard Events*

Name	Range	Description	Reference
twistY	[-30, 30]	This controls the rotation of each stripe pattern depending on its index in the matrix pattern. In *Chapter 6, Animating Parameters*, the slider's value is automated using data from the `eeg.txt` text file containing neural data recording.	*Chapter 3, Adding a GUI and Handling Keyboard Events*, and *Chapter 6, Animating Parameters*
pinchY	[0, 1]	This controls the scale of each stripe pattern depending on its index in the matrix pattern. In *Chapter 7, Distributed and Physical Computing with Networking and Arduino*, the slider's value is controlled by the `/pinchY` OSC command received from port `12345` and also by the Arduino device (using a potentiometer connected to Arduino's analog input **A0**).	*Chapter 3, Adding a GUI and Handling Keyboard Events*, and *Chapter 7, Distributed and Physical Computing with Networking and Arduino*

Global group

This group of sliders controls the position of the matrix pattern of the screen and also sets the background brightness:

Name	Range	Description	Reference
Scale	[0, 1]	Size of the matrix pattern on the screen	*Chapter 3, Adding a GUI and Handling Keyboard Events*
Rotate	[-180, 180]	Rotation of the matrix pattern on the screen in degrees	*Chapter 3, Adding a GUI and Handling Keyboard Events*
Background	[0, 255]	Brightness of the screen background	*Chapter 3, Adding a GUI and Handling Keyboard Events*

Primitive group

This group of sliders and checkboxes controls the drawing of the geometric primitives in the matrix pattern:

Name	Range	Description	Reference
shiftY	[-1000, 1000]	This controls the shift of each geometric primitive along its local *Y* axis.	*Chapter 3, Adding a GUI and Handling Keyboard Events*

Name	Range	Description	Reference
rotate	[-180, 180]	This controls the rotation of the local coordinate system of each geometric primitive.	*Chapter 3, Adding a GUI and Handling Keyboard Events*
size x, y	Two sliders, each in [0, 20]	This controls the width and height of each geometric primitive. This is not measured in pixels but as relative scaling. A value of 1 means no scaling.	*Chapter 3, Adding a GUI and Handling Keyboard Events*
color r, g, b, a	Four sliders, each in [0, 255]	This controls the color of each geometric primitive.	*Chapter 3, Adding a GUI and Handling Keyboard Events*
filled	Checkbox	If this checkbox is checked, then each geometric primitive is drawn as a filled figure. If not, only the contour of the primitive is drawn.	*Chapter 3, Adding a GUI and Handling Keyboard Events*
type	Checkbox	This switches between the rectangle (checked) and triangle (unchecked) shapes of each geometric primitive.	*Chapter 3, Adding a GUI and Handling Keyboard Events*

Mixer group

This group of sliders and checkboxes controls video mixing of images, video files, and live camera frame and also controls the kaleidoscope effect, mixing of layers with 2D and 3D graphics, and deformation of a sphere in 3D.

Name	Range	Description	Reference
image	[0, 255]	This controls the blending value for the `collage.png` image file.	*Chapter 4, Working with Raster Graphics – Images, Videos, and Shaders*
video	[0, 255]	This controls the blending value for the `flowing.mp4` video file.	*Chapter 4, Working with Raster Graphics – Images, Videos, and Shaders*
camera	[0, 255]	This controls the blending value for a live camera frame. The camera is disabled by default. To start it, press C.	*Chapter 4, Working with Raster Graphics – Images, Videos, and Shaders*
kenabled	Checkbox	This enables the kaleidoscope shader effect.	*Chapter 4, Working with Raster Graphics – Images, Videos, and Shaders*

Name	Range	Description	Reference
ksectors	1..100	This controls the number of kaleidoscope sectors.	*Chapter 4, Working with Raster Graphics – Images, Videos, and Shaders*
kangle	[-180, 180]	This controls the orientation of the circular sector, which is grabbed from the picture and repeated to obtain the kaleidoscope effect. In *Chapter 6, Animating Parameters*, the slider's value is automated; it linearly increases with time.	*Chapter 4, Working with Raster Graphics – Images, Videos, and Shaders*, and *Chapter 6, Animating Parameters*
kx	[0, 1]	This controls the relative *X* coordinate of the grabbed sector's vertex in the kaleidoscope effect. The value 0 means the left position, while the value 1 means the right position. In *Chapter 6, Animating Parameters*, the slider's value is automated using LFO based on the sine wave.	*Chapter 4, Working with Raster Graphics – Images, Videos, and Shaders*, and *Chapter 6, Animating Parameters*
ky	[0, 1]	This controls the relative *Y* coordinate of the grabbed sector's vertex in the kaleidoscope effect. The value 0 means the top position, while the value 1 means the bottom position.	*Chapter 4, Working with Raster Graphics – Images, Videos, and Shaders*
show2d	[0, 255]	This controls the blending value for the 2D picture obtained from the image, video, camera, and matrix pattern (processed with the kaleidoscope effect if enabled).	*Chapter 5, Creating 3D Graphics*
show3d	[0, 255]	This controls the blending value for the 3D image of the sphere.	*Chapter 5, Creating 3D Graphics*
rad	[0, 500]	This controls the radius of the sphere. In *Chapter 6, Animating Parameters*, the slider's value is automated using the sound level. The sound level is measured from the `skvo.wav` music track started by pressing *P* and also from the microphone (the results are summed up).	*Chapter 5, Creating 3D Graphics*, and *Chapter 6, Animating Parameters*
deform	[0, 1.5]	This controls the relative amplitude of the sphere's deformation by formulas. The value 0 gives no deformation, while the value 1 gives the deformation's amplitude equal to the sphere's radius.	*Chapter 5, Creating 3D Graphics*

Name	Range	Description	Reference
deformFreq	[0, 10]	This controls the space frequency of the sphere's deformation by analytical formulas. In *Chapter 6, Animating Parameters,* the slider's value is automated using LFO based on Perlin noise.	*Chapter 5, Creating 3D Graphics,* and *Chapter 6, Animating Parameters*
extrude	[0, 1]	This controls the relative amplitude of the sphere's extrusion based on the texture's brightness. The value 0 gives no extrusion, while the value 1 gives the maximal extrusion's amplitude equal to the sphere's radius.	*Chapter 5, Creating 3D Graphics*
automate	Checkbox	This enables the automation of the following sliders: `twistX`, `twistY`, `kangle`, `kx`, `rad`, and `deform`.	*Chapter 6, Animating Parameters*

iOS and Android versions

The video synthesizers for iOS and Android are light versions of the desktop project. They are considered in *Chapter 8, Deploying the Project on iOS, Android, and Raspberry Pi,* and include only the matrix pattern generator and the GUI panel. Instead of using the control keys, it uses the double-tap to toggle the GUI. Additionally, these projects use an accelerometer to control two sliders.

The openFrameworks project and source files

The project's code structure is the following:

- The project uses the `ofxGui` addon. It is linked to the project using the Pattern Generator wizard for the iOS version. For the Android version, the project is started by copying the example, which has already linked the `ofxGui` addon.
- The project's source files are `ofApp.h` and `ofApp.mm` for iOS and `ofApp.h` and `ofApp.cpp` for Android. They are placed in the `src` folder of the project.

Data files

The project writes and reads its GUI state to the `settings.xml` file.

The GUI

A GUI panel includes basic sliders and Global and Primitive groups described in the previous *The GUI controls* section under the *The desktop version* section.

Touches

A double-tap toggles the GUI visibility.

Accelerometer

The accelerometer values control the `twistX` and `twistY` sliders.

Raspberry Pi version

The video synthesizer for Raspberry Pi is a light version of the desktop project. It is considered in *Chapter 8, Deploying the Project on iOS, Android, and Raspberry Pi*.

This version is the same as the iOS and Android versions described earlier, with a small difference. It doesn't support the double-tap and the accelerometer but reacts to the *Esc*, *Z*, *Return* (*Enter*), *S*, and *L* keys, described in the *Control keys* section under the *The desktop version* section.

Summary

In this appendix, we considered an exhaustive reference on the desktop and mobile versions of our video synthesizer. It will be useful to you in the future to refresh your memory about using and modifying your video synthesizer.

B
openFrameworks Quick Reference

In this appendix, we have collected basic openFrameworks classes and functions, which were discussed in the book. The sections of the appendix are placed in the order in which the corresponding classes and functions appeared in the book. This appendix can act as a quick reminder on openFrameworks to write your own project.

Application

The `ofApp` class is the main class for the openFrameworks project. It is declared in the `ofApp.h` file, and its functions are defined in the `ofApp.cpp` file. It contains functions that are called by the openFrameworks engine on starting up, rendering, and various events from the user, such as mouse events and keyboard events. (See *Chapter 2, Creating Your First openFrameworks Project*, for details).

The most important functions that should be filled to have a working project are the following:

- `setup()`: This is called by openFrameworks once on starting the application. For example, it can include the following commands:

  ```
  ofSetWindowTitle( "My project" );
  ofSetWindowShape( 1280, 720 );
  ofSetFrameRate( 60 );
  ofSetFullScreen( true );
  ```

  The first line sets the application's window title to `My project`. The second line sets the window size to a width of 1280 pixels and a height of 720 pixels. The third line sets the rendering frame rate to 60 frames per second. The last line enables the fullscreen mode.

- `update()`: This is called for computations, such as processing the camera data.
- `draw()`: This is called to perform drawing onscreen.

The `update()` and `draw()` functions are called repeatedly until the application is stopped.

2D drawing

The basic drawing functions are the following (see *Chapter 2, Creating Your First openFrameworks Project*, for details):

Example of function usage	Description
`ofBackground( ofColor::white );`	This sets the background to the white color.
`float w = ofGetWidth();`	The `ofGetWidth()` function returns the current width of the application's screen in pixels. In this code, this value is set to the variable `w`.
`float h = ofGetHeight();`	The `ofGetHeight()` function returns the current height of the application's screen in pixels. In this code, this value is set to the variable `h`.
`ofLine( 100, 200, 300, 400 );`	This draws a line segment connecting the points (100, 200) and (300, 400).
`ofRect( 100, 200, 300, 400 );`	This draws a rectangle with the top-left corner (100, 200), a width of 300 pixels, and a height of 400 pixels. The `ofSetRectMode( OF_RECTMODE_CENTER )` command enables the mode for specifying the center of the rectangle instead of the top-left corner. The `ofSetRectMode( OF_RECTMODE_CORNER )` command enables the top-left corner mode back.
`ofTriangle( 10, 20, 30, 40, 50, 60 );`	This draws a triangle with the vertices (10, 20), (30, 40), and (50, 60).
`ofCircle( 100, 200, 30 );`	This draws a circle with the center (100, 200) and a radius of 30. The `ofSetCircleResolution( 10 )` command sets the circle resolution to 10, that is, the circle will be drawn consisting of 10 line segments.
`ofFill();`	This enables the mode for drawing filled figures.
`ofNoFill();`	This enables the mode for drawing unfilled figures.
`ofSetColor( 100, 150, 200 );`	This sets the drawing color with a red value of 100, a green value of 150, and a blue value of 200.

Example of function usage	Description
`ofSetColor(255,200);`	This sets the drawing color with the red, green, and blue values equal to 255 and the alpha value equal to 200. To enable additive blending, use the `ofEnableBlendMode( OF_BLENDMODE_ADD )` command. To enable alpha blending back, use the `ofEnableAlphaBlending()` command. (See *Chapter 4, Working with Raster Graphics – Images, Videos, and Shaders,* for details.)
`ofSetColor( ofColor::yellow );`	This sets the yellow drawing color.
`ofPushMatrix();`	This stores the current coordinate system to a special stack.
`ofPopMatrix();`	This restores the coordinate system from the stack.
`ofTranslate( 100, 200 );`	This translates the coordinate system by (200, 100) pixels.
`ofRotate( 90 );`	This rotates the coordinate system by 90 degrees clockwise.
`ofScale( 2, 2 );`	This scales the coordinate system; all objects will grow bigger by two times.

The GUI

The GUI is created using the `ofxGui` addon. Its basic classes are the following (see *Chapter 3, Adding a GUI and Handling Keyboard Events*, for details):

Class name with an example of an object definition	Description
`ofxPanel gui;`	This is a GUI panel, which can contain GUI controls, such as sliders, checkboxes, buttons, and also groups of GUI controls.
`ofxGuiGroup globalGroup;`	This is a group of GUI controls.
`ofxIntSlider countX;`	This is a slider with integer values.
`ofxFloatSlider stepX;`	This is a slider with float values.
`ofxVec2Slider size;`	This is a slider with two float values.
`ofxToggle filled;`	This is a checkbox.
`ofxColorSlider color;`	This is a color selector.

Multimedia and other classes

The following table lists the most important classes used in most openFrameworks projects. They are discussed in *Chapter 4, Working with Raster Graphics – Images, Videos, and Shaders, Chapter 5, Creating 3D Graphics, Chapter 6, Animating Parameters,* and *Chapter 7, Distributed and Physical Computing with Networking and Arduino.*

Class name with example of an object definition	**Description**
`ofImage image;`	This is an image class, which holds equal data in the RAM and video memory.
`ofPixels pixels;`	This is an image class, which holds data in RAM only.
`ofTexture texture;`	This is an image class, which holds data in video memory only.
`ofVideoPlayer video;`	This is a video player class.
`ofVideoGrabber camera;`	This a class for grabbing frames from a camera.
`ofFbo fbo;`	This is a buffer for offscreen drawing.
`ofShader shader;`	This is a shader class, which contains a vertex, fragment and, optionally, geometry shader programs.
`ofMesh mesh;`	This is a class for representing and drawing a set of primitives, such as triangles, lines, or points. The `ofEnableDepthTest()` command enables Z-buffering for proper drawing of 3D objects, and the `ofDisableDepthTest()` command disables it back.
`ofSpherePrimitive sphere;`	This is a class for representing and drawing a sphere in 3D. Also, there are the `ofPlanePrimitive`, `ofSpherePrimitive`, `ofIcoSpherePrimitive`, `ofCylinderPrimitive`, and `ofConePrimitive` classes for representing other simple geometrical objects.
`ofEasyCam cam;`	This is a camera for 3D drawing.
`ofLight light;`	This is the light source for 3D drawing.
`ofMaterial material;`	These are the material properties for 3D drawing.
`ofSoundPlayer sound;`	This is the sound player class.
`ofxOscReceiver oscReceiver;`	This is the receiver of OSC networking messages (it requires the `ofxOsc` addon).
`ofxOscSender oscSender;`	This is the sender of OSC networking messages (it requires the `ofxOsc` addon).
`ofSerial serial;`	This is the class for serial port communication with devices such as Arduino.

Mathematical, timer, and conversion functions

The mathematical, timer, and conversion functions were described in *Chapter 6, Animating Parameters*, and *Chapter 7, Distributed and Physical Computing with Networking and Arduino*, and are collected in this table:

Function	Description
`ofMap( x, 0, 1, 2, 3 )`	This linearly maps the float x from segment [0,1] to segment [2,3].
`ofMap( x, 0, 1, 2, 3, true )`	This linearly maps the float x from the segment [0,1] to the segment [2,3], clamping the output value to the [2,3] range (it occurs when x is not in segment [0,1]).
`ofClamp( x, 0, 1 )`	This clamps the float x to the range [0,1].
`ofInRange( x, 0, 1 )`	This returns `true` if the float x lies in the segment [0,1] and returns `false` in the opposite case.
`ofToString( 0.5 )`	This converts a numeric value (integer or float) to a string.
`ofGetElapsedTime()`	This is the number of seconds elapsed from the application start; the returned value is float.
`ofNoise( x )`	This is the Perlin noise value for float x.
`ofToFloat( "0.5" )`	This converts a string to a float number.
`ofToInt( "5" )`	This converts a string to an integer.

`vector<string> list = ofSplitString( "aa;bb;cc;dd", ";" );`	This splits a string into an array of strings. The first argument is the string, and the second argument is the delimeter. In our example, the resulting array list will consist of the four elements:
	`list[0] = "aa"`
	`list[1] = "bb"`
	`list[2] = "cc"`
	`list[3] = "dd"`

Summary

We listed a short description of the main application class, 2D drawing functions, GUI, and multimedia classes and even of the mathematical functions discussed in the book. For detailed information, see the corresponding chapters.

Note that openFrameworks contains much more useful functions, classes, and addons than are mentioned in our book. So, if you require some feature you are unable to find in the appendix and in the whole book, search for it in the openFrameworks examples, documentation, addons list, forum, or books (see *Chapter 9, Further Resources*, for details).

Index

Symbols

A

C

L

M

N

O

P

R

S

T

U

V

W

Z

Thank you for buying
openFrameworks Essentials

About Packt Publishing

Packt, pronounced 'packed', published its first book, *Mastering phpMyAdmin for Effective MySQL Management*, in April 2004, and subsequently continued to specialize in publishing highly focused books on specific technologies and solutions.

Our books and publications share the experiences of your fellow IT professionals in adapting and customizing today's systems, applications, and frameworks. Our solution-based books give you the knowledge and power to customize the software and technologies you're using to get the job done. Packt books are more specific and less general than the IT books you have seen in the past. Our unique business model allows us to bring you more focused information, giving you more of what you need to know, and less of what you don't.

Packt is a modern yet unique publishing company that focuses on producing quality, cutting-edge books for communities of developers, administrators, and newbies alike. For more information, please visit our website at `www.packtpub.com`.

About Packt Open Source

In 2010, Packt launched two new brands, Packt Open Source and Packt Enterprise, in order to continue its focus on specialization. This book is part of the Packt Open Source brand, home to books published on software built around open source licenses, and offering information to anybody from advanced developers to budding web designers. The Open Source brand also runs Packt's Open Source Royalty Scheme, by which Packt gives a royalty to each open source project about whose software a book is sold.

Writing for Packt

We welcome all inquiries from people who are interested in authoring. Book proposals should be sent to `author@packtpub.com`. If your book idea is still at an early stage and you would like to discuss it first before writing a formal book proposal, then please contact us; one of our commissioning editors will get in touch with you.

We're not just looking for published authors; if you have strong technical skills but no writing experience, our experienced editors can help you develop a writing career, or simply get some additional reward for your expertise.

Mastering openFrameworks: Creative Coding Demystified

ISBN: 978-1-84951-804-8 Paperback: 364 pages

A practical guide to creating audiovisual interactive projects with low-level data processing using openFrameworks

1. Create cutting edge audio-visual interactive projects, interactive installations, and sound art projects with ease.
2. Unleash the power of low-level data processing methods using C++ and shaders.
3. Make use of the next generation technologies and techniques in your projects involving OpenCV, Microsoft Kinect, and so on.

Kinect for Windows SDK Programming Guide

ISBN: 978-1-84969-238-0 Paperback: 392 pages

Build motion-sensing applications with Microsoft's Kinect for Windows SDK quickly and easily

1. Building application using Kinect for Windows SDK.
2. Covers the Kinect for Windows SDK v1.6.
3. A practical step-by-step tutorial to make learning easy for a beginner.
4. A detailed discussion of all the APIs involved and the explanations of their usage in detail.

Cinder – Begin Creative Coding

ISBN: 978-1-84951-956-4 Paperback: 146 pages

A quick introduction into the world of creative coding with Cinder through basic tutorials and a couple of advanced examples

1. More power - Cinder is one of the most powerful creative coding engines out there and it will be hard to find a better one for your professional grade project.
2. Do it fast - each section should not take longer than one hour to complete.
3. We give you the tools and it is up to you what you do with them - we won't go into complicated algorithms, but rather give you the brushes and paints so you can paint the way you already know.

Processing 2: Creative Coding HOTSHOT

ISBN: 978-1-78216-672-6 Paperback: 266 pages

Learn Processing with exciting and engaging projects to make your computer talk, see, hear, express emotions, and even design physical objects

1. Teach your computer to create physical objects, visualize data, and program a custom hardware controller.
2. Create projects that can be run on a variety of platforms, ranging from desktop computers to Android smartphones.
3. Each chapter presents a complete project and guides you through the implementation using easy-to-follow, step-by-step instructions.

Made in the USA
Middletown, DE
15 November 2016